Praise fo

M000078311

"Timothy Snyder's *Lived Vocatic* als and those without any formal theological training to rethink our assumptions about what it means to work. By centering the real stories of everyday people, Snyder invites readers into a thoughtful and neces- sary reflection on our theological assumptions about vocation. In a time when the very idea of vocation is regularly debated, this work offers a grounded interlocutor who helps us collectively and prophetically reimagine one of our most fundamental practices."

—Rev. Dr. Timothy L. Adkins-Jones, assistant professor of homiletics, Union Theological Seminary, and senior pastor, Bethany Baptist Church, Newark, New Jersey

"Not only does Snyder reenvision a theology of vocation that fits with our present ways of working; he gives life to a way of doing theology that involves listening to people's stories with openness and humility. I love the room Snyder leaves to say, 'I don't know.' I love his suggestion that theology needs to learn the art of improvisation. *Lived Vocation* inspires the reader to author their own narrative rather than submit to scripts imposed from the top down. A compelling and excellent read."

—Rev. Debbie Blue, pastor, House of Mercy, St. Paul, Minnesota, and author of *Sensual Orthodoxy*, *Consider the Women*, and *From Stone to Living Word*

"Snyder is a theological Studs Terkel. He has crafted a compelling inter- pretation of work that pays close attention to the promise and pain of work as well as to the people who do the work. The result is a beautiful interweaving of story and theology, testimony and tradition. A model of how theology is done in community, always connected to Christian life."

—Dr. David H. Jensen, academic dean and professor in the Clarence N. and Betty B. Frierson Distinguished Chair of Reformed Theology, Austin Presbyterian Theological Seminary, and author of *Responsive Labor: A Theology of Work*

"Snyder's book is a testimony to the power of story to create lives of meaning. In and through this testimony he encourages the reader to focus on the 'how' and the 'why' of work more than the 'what,' and challenges the church (especially those of us whose work is that of doing theology) to move toward a descriptive theology that sees our individual and collective stories as the source material we need to see God's ongoing creative activity in the world."

—Rev. Dr. Mindy Makant, director, Living Well Center
for Vocation and Purpose, Lenoir-Rhyne University

"Alive with stories, *Lived Vocation* offers a rare glimpse into the beautifully complex lives of people in diverse forms of work. The stories are rich in detail and practical wisdom, based on interviews with farmers, teachers, merchants, health care givers, hairdressers, homemakers, and more. Snyder uncovers patterns and differences in human understandings and practices of work, and thus expands on Christian theologies of vocation. The book is a joy to read, and it will, as Snyder promises, change you."

—Dr. Mary Elizabeth Moore, dean emerita and professor emerita of
theology and education, Boston University School of Theology

"Snyder shares the multifaceted lived experiences of real people at work, challenging our default understanding of the vocations of others. Meanwhile, he models how their witness unveiled for him the complexity of his own sense of vocation."

—Rev. Dr. Phil Ruge-Jones, director of the Lay School of Ministry for the
Northwest Synod of Wisconsin; pastor of Grace Lutheran Church, Eau
Claire, Wisconsin; and author of *The Word of the Cross in a World of Glory*

"Snyder has written one of the most honest and remarkable theologies of work I've read. Appropriately, as a Lutheran practical theologian studying Lutheran congregations and their membership, he draws on a rich theological tradition that comes down from Martin Luther on the value and dignity of daily work. His close-to-the-ground stories from everyday Christians are the heart of the book, and his brilliant engagement with them opens up a vibrant vision of how to imagine God involved in the place where most of us spend the majority of our lives. While his stories are from Lutherans of European background, an unsurprising fact given that the Evangelical Lutheran Church in America is predominantly white, his rich canvas of stories ought to inspire others, from other traditions and backgrounds, to add their stories and thereby deepen the rich and rewarding path upon which this work embarks."

—Rev. Christian Scharen, pastor, St. Lydia's
Dinner Church, Brooklyn, New York

LIVED VOCATION

LIVED VOCATION

STORIES OF FAITH AT WORK

TIMOTHY K. SNYDER

FORTRESS PRESS
MINNEAPOLIS

LIVED VOCATION
Stories of Faith at Work

Cover design and illustration by Paul Soupiset

Print ISBN: 978-1-5064-8134-0
eBook ISBN: 978-1-5064-8135-7

For mom & dad —
whose life's work has been us four boys.

Contents

Preface

This book is a collection of stories about everyday work. All the stories included were shared with me between September 2017 and December 2018, but they do not belong to me. They belong to those who shared them with me during interviews I conducted for a research study. They are teachers, bank executives, farmers, healthcare workers, real estate agents, mechanics, and more. All the people I interviewed had worked for decades. I, on the other hand, had only begun my career as a professional theologian—which is, to be honest, a very strange job.

I set out to interview these workers because I wanted to know if and how faith shows up in the world of work today. Most of all, I wanted to know what difference Christian faith made in the midst of everyday lives. As we spend so much of our time at work, I figured that was a good place to start. So I identified three very different communities for the interviews: a large city that serves as its state's capital, a former industrial town trying to reimagine itself for the twenty-first century, and a small, agriculturally centered town—the kind where most people know everyone by name. I then reached out to Lutheran churches (because I am Lutheran), and after explaining my project, I asked their pastors to provide a list of potential participants.

Though I did not ask this specifically, I am confident most of those I interviewed thought this was a strange project. While there may be exceptions, most of us do not think our lives are all that exceptional. Why would a professional theologian want to interview me? Actually, I showed up to each interview with a very particular bias. I came convinced that God was already at work in their lives whether they knew that or not. My job was to listen carefully and hope I might capture that.

While I expected to learn from their experiences of work today, I did not foresee that their stories would change how I thought about *my work* as a theologian. But that is exactly what happened. Before I met these workers, I thought about the work of theology as translation work. The job of a theologian was to translate the wisdom of our traditions in way that would make sense for contemporary Christians. Or to put it differently, theologians were stewards and ambassadors of theological truth, and it was our job to help others see what the tradition has to offer. After these interviews, I still see my work as translation work, but now in the opposite direction. The work of theology is not to rehearse the great classics of the tradition. Rather, the task is to improvise with this faith that has been passed down generation to generation. More deserves to be said about this shift from a "classical Christianity" to "improvisational Christianity," but first, a few words about what the following stories can and cannot offer.

The Power of Everyday Stories

The power of these stories is found in what they offer collectively. It is not enough for theologians to engage contemporary life with anecdotes from our own lives. We theologians must be grounded in the stories of other ordinary Christians, especially those who have had very different lives than ours. From his prison cell in Nazi Germany, Lutheran theologian and pastor Dietrich Bonhoeffer wrote a brief essay called "What It Means to Tell the Truth." Back then he wrote that truth-telling was not always self-evident. Instead, it required a long and discerning engagement with the concrete realities and struggles of everyday life.[1]

---

1 Dietrich Bonhoeffer, *Conspiracy and Imprisonment, 1940–1945*, Dietrich Bonhoeffer Works, vol. 16. Mark Brocker, ed., Lisa Dahill, trans. (Minneapolis: Fortress), 601–608.

Bonhoeffer's writing from prison seems to resonate with one of Martin Luther's most well-known claims hundreds of years before him. Writing about the difference between two kinds of theology, Luther wrote that a *theologian of glory* calls a good thing bad and a bad thing good, but a *theologian of the cross* calls a thing what it is.[2] Both of these theologians saw that theology begins and ends with its ability to take root in our actual lives as they *really* are. This book offers a modest but uncommon window into that kind of theology through the everyday world of work.

At the beginning, when I said that this is a collection of stories, I really should have said that it is a *curated* collection of stories. This is not every story these ordinary workers shared with me, and none of their individual stories are told from beginning to end. Instead, they have been arranged thematically. The first set of stories are origin stories. They tell stories about how these workers came to their work in the first place. The second set of stories is about the daily grind of their work. Just as the Genesis story says, our work is labor that takes a toll on us (see Genesis 3:17–19). The third and final set of stories tells why work can still be meaningful for ordinary people of faith.

This invitation to think about everyday storytelling brings us back to the work of theology. There was a time when theology was considered the "queen of the sciences," and to be a student of theology was to be in pursuit of knowledge that was above all the rest. It was the pursuit of ultimate truth. It is not a mistake that this idea came to the foreground during a time when the church had the kind of visibility and political power to enforce its doctrines. At times, the church violently enforced its understanding of theology.

Even though the church can no longer enforce its teachings with the sword, it has continued to use other manipulative means,

---

2   Martin Luther, "Heidelberg Disputation, 1518" in *Luther's Works*, American ed., vol. 31, Harold J. Grimm and Helmut T. Lehman eds. (Philadelphia: Fortress), 40.

such as guilt and shame, to ensure its orthodoxy. Some readers will come to this book thinking this is all in the past because they have had very positive experiences at church. For others, however, this will hit a little too close to home because they have experienced that the church can still be a bully. That alone should be enough to get all of us theologians to rethink what kind of influence theology should have in our everyday lives.

Some of my colleagues no doubt will see what I am about to say as going too far. But only slightly removed from the use of swords and shame to enforce theology's authority is the notion that theology is *normative*. What I mean by this is that most theology makes claims about how ordinary believers (those who are not formally trained theologians) *ought* to understand matters of faith—how we *ought* to understand our lives. The stories that follow have made me question that entire way of thinking about the work of theology, and I am convinced we need to find new ways of doing this work.

I came to this project with a genuine belief that the Protestant theology of vocation offered an invaluable resource for understanding how we might serve God in everyday life. I was, of course, not alone in that belief. There are quite literally dozens of books on vocation that make exactly that case. I read those books and thought I understood how to think theologically about work today.

But then something happened.

As I listened to the stories these workers shared, some indeed did fit what I will call throughout this book the "vocational script." Their experiences matched the story that theology tells about the relationship between God's work and ours. Other stories, however, did not seem to fit. My first instinct was to reframe such stories in ways that would make them less problematic for how I understood vocation. The more I read and reread them, however, I started to think that perhaps it was not the workers and their stories that needed to be changed to fit the theology. Rather, our theology needs to take into account the wisdom of people's actual experiences. This book is a collection of stories about work that invites the church to reconsider how we think theologically about our everyday lives.

Cautionary Notes

Before going any further, it is important to offer several *cautionary notes* about the collection of stories you are about to read. These notes provide context about the steps that were taken to collect these stories, and they outline the risks and responsibilities that researchers (like me) assume when we share the stories of our research participants. Most importantly, these stories were collected as part of a larger dissertation research project in a doctoral program at Boston University.

Because of this context, I took several steps that have become standard in theologically informed qualitative research, including:

1. Submitting all my research plans in advance for review by the University's Institutional Review Board. IRBs play an important role in ensuring that research involving other people is done ethically.
2. Developing clear criteria about who was "eligible" for participation in my study and who was not. Because of my scholarly focus at the time, I limited my study to adults between the ages of 55–65 who were also members of the Evangelical Lutheran Church in America.
3. Designing a process for recruiting that relied on local pastors and their knowledge of their congregants. I met with pastors who then, in turn, introduced me to potential research participants.
4. Using a process of "informed consent" with all my research participants. That process involved informing participants

in advance of how I would be using their stories and seeking their permission to use their stories in my future scholarly work.

5. Protecting the identities of all my participants using pseudonyms. The names included in this book have been changed to protect their privacy.

The context of formal research also created three additional realities that are vital knowledge for readers:

This study is a small-scale project.
Therefore, it is a limited sample.
And yet, it is the beginning of a collection of stories, not the end.

Each of these realities deserves further elaboration because each one offers important context about what can and cannot be said collectively about the stories you are about to encounter.

Qualitative Research in Theology

Qualitative research has its origins in the social sciences, but in recent decades, theologians have increasingly turned to these methods to explore lived faith, the practice of ministry, and the church. This kind of research is much more time-consuming than traditional theological research. For doctoral students, taking on a dissertation that involves qualitative research can often add one to two years to the length of their program. It can take months to recruit participants and schedule interviews. Countless hours are spent creating transcripts, and even more hours are then spent analyzing what can be thousands of pages of data. All of that happens before a single page is written to explain what a researcher has actually learned.

Because this work is extraordinarily complex and time-consuming, and because there are time limits associated with a doctoral program, qualitative studies in theology are often limited to small-scale studies of a dozen or two dozen participants. This was certainly my experience.

Large-scale studies involving hundreds of participants have the advantage of *breadth*. They can include a wide variety of experiences across an entire region, or even across the country. But small-scale studies have their advantages too. Small-scale studies have the advantage of *depth*. They can follow the experiences of participants over time through multiple interviews. Both are an important part of how researchers learn from the experiences of others.

Even though I know all researchers must make difficult decisions within the limits of their time and resources, I constantly wondered whether I had enough data, whether I should do more interviews or collect more audio journals, and whether I had anything important to say about the data I had collected. In the end I was comforted by the way another qualitative researcher describes the goal of data collection: "when you don't learn anything new for a while, your study is complete."[3] I reached that point in the spring of 2018 after recruiting eighteen participants from three very different communities.

The Limits of this Collection

Readers will quickly realize that as a collection of stories, many things are missing. This is not a complete picture of work today. Who is and who is not included in any research sample is always a dilemma—and one for which there is no easy solution. We qualitative researchers always want the most diverse sample of participants we can possibly recruit. However, we can only work with those who actually agree to participate, and even then it is challenging, if not impossible, to achieve the ideal research sample.

---

3 Howard S. Becker, *Evidence* (Chicago: University of Chicago Press, 2017), 173.

In the end my collection of stories of everyday work was limited in three particular ways.

For example, all eighteen of these workers come from families of European descent. This is not terribly surprising given that participants were recruited from churches affiliated with the Evangelical Lutheran Church in America (ELCA)—a denomination that is 96 percent white.[4] As a part of my recruitment process, I approached two ELCA congregations whose congregations were predominantly people of color (one African American and one Latinx). However, due to scheduling conflicts, neither pastor was able to commit at the time of the study.

Similarly, while these workers come from a range of socioeconomic backgrounds, they lean toward the kind of privileged narratives we might expect from those whose work does indeed meet all their basic needs. This, too, is not surprising given the broader membership of the ELCA. According to a 2016 report from the Pew Forum, about 19 percent of ELCA members reported earning less than $30,000 annually, 22 percent reported earning between $30,000–$49,000 annually, another 32 percent reported earning between $50,000–$99,999, and just 26 percent reported earning over $100,000.[5] These figures map almost identically onto what my research participants reported.

Finally, while I was surprised that my eventual sample of research participants included a wide range of work, many other kinds of work are not included in the collection. For example, no one in my sample worked a minimum wage job, no one worked within the so-called "gig economy," and my selection criteria ensured that no religious professionals were included in the study. In short, this collection of stories—like all qualitative research

---

4 https://www.pewresearch.org/religion/religious-landscape-study/religious-denomination/evangelical-lutheran-church-in-america-elca/#demographic-information

5 https://www.pewresearch.org/fact-tank/2016/10/11/how-income-varies-among-u-s-religious-groups/.

studies—simply is not everything that needs to be said about the world of work today. Fortunately, as a researcher, I know that research builds on research, and even small-scale studies can yield important insights and demonstrate the need for future research. No study ever tells the whole story.

Personally, I still struggle with the limits of research like this. As a teacher I am constantly trying to provide my students with the widest range of perspectives possible, and I regularly warn my students about the dangers of viewing the world through the perspectives and experiences of those who are in privileged places of power (perspectives and experiences that look a whole lot like, well, me and many of my students). There is a real risk in studies like this one where researchers can end up simply confirming their own preconceived conclusion, or worse, they can end up amplifying voices that already occupy places of privilege.

But that is the paradox of generating new knowledge and insights from very particular experiences. As practical theologian Eileen Campbell-Reed has put it, "The paradox of using single or small numbers of case studies is that although human beings need single cases for understanding the complexity and intensity of a situation, single cases are constantly suspect because of their limitations, perceived or real bias, and their novelty."[6] In today's data-driven world, it is tempting to think that the only kind of knowledge that matters is generalizable knowledge—the kind that is universally true independent from the context of that knowledge. But as Campbell-Reed points out, that is *not* the only kind of knowledge we need to live faithfully in this world God has given us. We also need context-dependent knowledge—the kind of knowledge that can only be learned in practice over time. And that is exactly what is at the heart of this collection of stories. It is a

---

6   Eileen Campbell-Reed, "The Power and Danger of a Single Case Study in Practical Theological Research" in *Conundrums in Practical Theology*, ed. Joyce Ann Mercer and Bonnie J. Miller McLemore (Leiden: Brill, 2016), 38.

collection of stories about the practical wisdom needed to navigate the complex intersection of lived faith and contemporary work.

How to Read This Book

I wrote this book with two audiences in mind: professional religious leaders and ordinary people of faith. All readers should know a few things before proceeding.

First of all, unlike other books, I am not trying to persuade you to think about the world of work like I do. You are not about to walk onto the stage of a theological debate. Instead, imagine a very different kind of stage—a place where you will encounter many different characters and where you will hear many different voices. Their stories and your experience of them *is the point*. On this stage you will hear testimonies.

Second, this book is best consumed like a fine wine. I recommend that you sip, not gulp. The stories are told through short essays of just a few pages. Try reading two or three at a time and then take a break. I especially recommend reading these with others. I think you will be surprised how others hear things you may have missed. Some of your favorite stories will probably be the ones that turned others off and vice versa. All of that, too, *is the point*.

To my readers who are professional religious leaders: Before you go on, I must ask you to do something very difficult. I have to ask you to temporarily forget all your theological training and experience. These have given you "eyes to see" and "ears to hear" as the Scriptures say. That is a gift most of the time, but this is not one of them. If possible, I want to invite you to take on what contemplatives call *the beginner's mind*. Try to hear these stories as you would have heard them long before you became a professional religious leader. The reason I ask this is simple. You likely already think about your work as a vocation or as a calling. Your training provided you the language, the occasion, and an entire professional community of folks who talk about their work this way. But this is not the norm; this collection of stories does not depend on such theological presuppositions.

To my readers who are not professional religious leaders: Thank you for picking up a theology book. I am not sure I would do the same if I were you. I hope the stories you read will remind you of episodes and memories from your own working life. I hope you will reconnect with those stories that you tell often and those that you have forgotten about until now. If you are up for it, I hope you will share your story with others. If nothing else, I hope you will see your story is just the kind of source material that we theologians need to hear in order to understand God's ongoing work in the world. At this moment in history, we theologians may need you far more than you need us.

Proceed with caution.

These stories might change you.

They changed me.

I

The World of Work Today

> Then the Lord God said, "See, the man has become like one of us, knowing good and evil; and now, he might reach out his hand and take also from the tree of life, and eat, and live forever"—therefore the Lord God sent him forth from the garden of Eden, to till the ground from which he was taken. He drove out the man; and at the east of the garden of Eden he placed the cherubim, and a sword flaming and turning to guard the way to the tree of life.
>
> —Genesis 3:22–25, NRSV

Life is difficult to imagine without work.

Here and now, we live "east of Eden," and our very lives *are* work. Despite the ubiquitous place it has in our lives, work itself is difficult to define. *What, exactly, counts as work and what does not?* Answering such a question in any definitive way seems like some kind of arcane philosophical exercise, such as trying to define the meaning of life. Yet the demands of our working lives are never further from us than the sound of the weekday alarm clock or the sound of an infant's cry in the middle of the night. Work, whether of the eight-to-five variety or the unpaid labor of love variety, is always calling.

According to Genesis, the story of work is as old as creation itself. As that story goes, there was a time when we humans did not have to work, but after the Fall, work became part of living. Originally, God had intended a different kind of partnership between our work and his, but when Adam violated the boundaries God had set for us, the very nature of work changed. Work became toil, and our lives became labor. Our work may continue to be a collaboration with God, but this does not overshadow the harsh realities of work. Genesis is quite clear: work is difficult, and it will take its toll on all of us (see Genesis 3).

For all of history, our work has been a defining feature of human life—both who we are individually and who we are together in society. Yet even if work is difficult to define, one thing has been consistently true about our working lives: work is always changing; it evolves alongside our own development. Let's begin our exploration of the world of work today by taking a brief tour through the history of human work.

A Brief History of Work

The first thing that must be said about the world of work is that, for the vast majority of human history, work was done in small groups of no more than a few households. All shared in the work and all shared equally in its fruits. Some historians suggest that if you were to map the history of working on a timeline, this kind of shared work would make up 98 percent of human history. Work's development into what we experience today is a relatively new thing. Even though the focus of this book is not on economics or ethics, it is important to note that today we take inequality among working lives as a matter of fact, as an irreversible or even pre-ordained reality. But this has not always been the case and often today our working lives do not reflect God's intentions for us to live life and to live it abundantly (see John 10:10).

We begin to see important changes to our working lives with the "invention" of farming, a period historians refer to as the Neolithic Revolution. Over time, yields produced surpluses and that created the possibility of trading one's leftover goods for other needs and wants. And once such surpluses were reliable, we begin to see a division of labor, and professional specialization increased.

Some workers could focus on producing crops and livestock for a much larger population, while other workers could focus their time and energy on other kinds of work.

Some labor historians have suggested that, in some important ways, this is the entire story. Once the groundwork was laid for a division of labor, it was only a matter of time until our working lives would unfold into the complex modern version of society we find today. There is no doubt that much of what we experience today can be traced to these developments thousands of years ago, but it is not quite the full story.

When agriculture became widespread and the domestication of livestock created the possibility of surpluses, two related developments followed: the marketplace and the city-state. Early efforts at trading goods took place through bartering, and while this practice continues even today, monetary markets eventually became the norm. This led to the possibility of expanding trade across cultures and societies. It is around this time that we see the emergence of the earliest cities, often located along strategic trade routes and ports. Monetized markets created new forms of work altogether, such as self-employment and wage labor—both of which continue to be an important part of today's world of work.

During this period, we find several significant shifts in labor relations. First, the number of professions increased from perhaps just a dozen or so to as many as a hundred. It would be difficult to underestimate how the division of labor and specialization continue to shape our working lives even as they change at rapid pace. Another important shift occurred as, across cultures, work became engendered, meaning some things became thought of as "men's work" and other things became thought of as "women's work"—a dynamic that may have been pragmatically driven at one point, but is often today a source of profound injustice.

The period between 5000 and 500 BCE produced some of the earliest civilizations, such as those that sprung up in the Fertile Crescent and in the Indus, Yellow, and Yangtze River valleys. Eventually, these civilizations centralized efforts to organize work and redistribute the production they yielded. But this growth depended on a third kind of labor relation beyond self-employment and wage labor: *enslaved* labor. The growth of these civilizations would not have been possible were it not for subjugation of thousands of workers. And, of course, it would not be the last time that social progress and economic success for some were achieved at the expense of others.

As cities grew into city-states and even larger societies, some began to grow in their economic and political capacity, or what we now call globalization. Around 1500 CE, much of the world was still made up of large geographic and economic islands. Cultural exchange and trade were limited within each continent. The turning point can be found in the technological innovations that made cross-continental maritime travel possible. Before this point, on nearly every continent, one could still find communities of hunter-gathers living alongside agriculturally oriented societies. But once permanent contact between continents was established, we see the rapid demise of hunter-gathers.

Historians and other scholars agree that the most significant set of changes to our working lives can be traced to the Industrial Revolution. While the exact beginning of the Industrial Revolution continues to be debated by scholars, by the mid-1700s, its impact was clear in Britain. Further developments, however, would take the next two hundred years to unfold. Part of what makes the Industrial Revolution such a defining event for the world of work today is that the process of globalization emerged alongside it.

The Industrial Revolution brought with it a series of changes to labor, the economy, and even daily life. Driving the changes to labor included new manufacturing and technological innovations that increased the scale and productivity of key industries, such as textiles and iron. Large-scale factories became much more common, creating new opportunities for wage labor. Unfortunately, many factory workers included unmarried women, children, and orphans—all vulnerable populations easy to exploit.

It is true that the Industrial Revolution would eventually lead to unprecedented improvements in the standard of living for a significant part of industrialized nations. But it would take several hundred years before that impact was realized. Consider that between 1800 and 1913, worldwide trade grew fivefold. As late as the early twentieth century, unemployment in the United States was regularly around 20 percent. Child labor was common, and while new laws attempted to ensure workplace safety, the only real recourse against dangerous working conditions were lawsuits, which were rarely successful. The costs endured for the Industrial Revolution's eventual progress were steep.

Alongside industrialization, we find significant changes to transportation, communication, and cultural exchange—forces that drove globalization. By the turn of the twentieth century, the world itself was increasingly becoming a frame of reference for the experiences of everyday life. As literacy rates grew in Europe, Asia, and the Middle East, mass media and journalism brought ideas and news across the world. By the turn of the century, a vast rail network connected Europe to Asia, and steam-powered ships dominated the seas. Together these created new trade opportunities, increased travel, and exposure to other cultures. While personal travel was still a luxury of the privileged elite, the growth in travel led to increased global awareness of other people and places. It was during this period that one could start to imagine a *world* economy or a *world* community of nations.

These twin developments—the Industrial Revolution and globalization—created vast new economic opportunities, but they also created a new scale of economic hardship along the way. Because the positive impacts of these developments were not evenly distributed, ordinary workers often turned to their political leaders for new kinds of interventions. In Britain and Europe, workers organized together through trade unions to demand the government introduce new regulations to their working conditions. Soon, however, the state would not only regulate our working lives; rather, governments themselves became significant economic actors. For example, during the Civil War, the United States government leveraged northern industries to support the war effort and the wartime economy. Today, local and national governments continue to regulate our working lives and to contribute to economic life through employment, government spending, and investment. It is important to remember that while we take for granted that our government is an active player in our working lives, this was not always the case.

Several additional changes to the nature of work are notable after the Industrial Revolution. First, workers increasingly found themselves working under the direct supervision of an employer. The possibility of self-employment, once common in pre-industrialization economies, decidedly decreased. Motivation to work and to work hard was now the responsibility of managers. A new managerial class of workers took on the responsibilities of planning the work, the development of the industry, and the structure of compensation. Testimonies from workers during this time reveal a workforce that was proud of its work, but that also yearned for better conditions and a greater share of the economy's unprecedented growth.

In the middle of this most recent era, abolition movements transformed the world of work. Today, we may take for granted the immorality of slavery, but it is important to remember that in places such as Britain and France, it was not until the early nineteenth century that the abolition of slavery was codified into law. In the United States, it would take the Civil War to decide the fate of enslaved persons. And it was not until 1948 that slavery was declared illegal in the Universal Declaration of Human Rights.

The history of work, even as briefly outlined here, tells a story of work's continuous evolution. The world of work has undergone extraordinary changes over time, and we should expect nothing less going forward. Whenever and however work changes, historically we see the benefits of those changes unevenly distributed so that some benefit, and often those benefits come at the expense of others. Several themes have come to shape our world of work in enduring ways, including the relationship between employers and employees, the rights of workers, the role of the state in the economy, and a global stage that shapes nearly every kind of work today.

One way to think about work—both a working life and the role work plays in our broader society—is to consider when work begins and when work ends. Most of us remember when we started working. We remember that first job. Though not everyone will find it possible, we still expect that most workers will eventually retire and not *have to* work. Because our working lives grow and develop throughout our life cycle, the story of our work is often closely related to our families of origin and our educational experiences.

At home we often internalize our earliest imaginations of what counts as "good work." Some may embrace the family business or follow in the footsteps of a parent or sibling. Others may do the exact opposite, yet both illustrate the important role our families of origin play in shaping our working lives. More than ever, the possibilities and limits one faces at work are tied to qualifications and credentials obtained from educational institutions. In school and university settings, we are introduced to those who are like us and those who are not. Among them are peers and mentors who often have an extraordinary impact on us and the careers that follow. In our schooling, we are trained to think about our work in certain ways, and we learn foundational practices that accompany us for the rest of our lives. Today, for many middle- to upper-class Americans, college is not just about the formal education we receive; it is a rite of passage into adulthood and the inauguration of our working lives.

Thinking about these influences on our working lives leads to an important issue for the world of work today: the notion of *choice*. It is true, of course, that in some sense, we do indeed choose the work we do. And that alone is important because that has not always been true throughout human history. In fact, it is a relatively new phenomenon. However, like other aspects of everyday life, we make these choices within the limits of what we know about a field of work, the skills and abilities we possess, our motivation to accomplish that work, and the availability of positions. These limits are all part of what it means to work within modern, globalized market capitalist societies. At nearly every turn, the stories that follow reflect this reality of life lived within limits.

So what do we make of our working lives? What stories do we tell ourselves and others about the meaning or significance of our work? That is exactly what this book is about. It is a book about ordinary people of faith and their efforts to relate the meaning of their work to their lives of faith. As you will soon see, this intersection of faith and work is much more complicated than we often assume. At other points in human history, it may have been easier to integrate faith and daily life. And today, some professions may be easier to integrate in this way than others. But our working lives are extraordinarily complex, and the relationship between faith and work cannot easily be assumed or taken for granted.

Before we get to the stories, it is important to know something about the contexts and settings in which these stories of work take place. It is also important to note that all the names below, along with many details, have been changed in order to protect the privacy of those who participated in the study. In every case, the participants provided their informed consent to be interviewed and to have their stories included in settings such as this.[1]

---

1 The research study on which this book is based, "Vocation, Work, and Late Adulthood," including all its procedures, underwent an ethics review by the Charles River Campus Institutional Review Board at Boston University.

Work at the Office

For many of us, going to work means going to the office. Across nearly every industry and including a wide range of jobs, the office itself has become the place that shapes our imagination about work. "The office" is synonymous with nine-to-five schedules, desks, chairs, computer workstations, cubicles (or if you're lucky, maybe even a private office), organizational charts, conference rooms, the cursed copy machine that no one really knows how to work, and, of course, paperwork and emails.

When Karl Marx wrote about alienation,[2] he had in mind the work that takes place on factory floors. Yet work at the office has its own kind of alienation, marked by mundane repetition, specialized tasks, and opaque bureaucratic processes that distance us from the products we create and the services that we provide. Many of the workers whom you will meet in the pages that follow work in offices. They come from a range of industries and sectors, but their places of work share much in common.

The city planner

A civil engineer by training, James is a city planner who has worked for the local government for the past fourteen years. Early

---

2 By "alienation," Marx was describing how industrialization had fundamentally changed the relationship between workers and their work. The heart of the matter can be captured in this line from Marx: "[The worker] is at home when he is not working, and when he is working he is not at home." The full description of alienation can be found in Marx's Economic-Philosophical Manuscripts of 1844. See Karl Marx, *The Portable Karl Marx*, Eugene Kamenka, ed. (New York: Penguin Books, 1983), 132–46.

on he worked in the private sector, but a colleague recruited him to work for the city years ago.

At the office, James is known as the person who will actually field phone calls from local citizens. When he is not on the phone, he has plenty of paperwork—an occupational hazard for government employees.

Even though James has an office at city hall, he is not always there. Often on the way into the office, he will stop by project sites. For example, a new roundabout is going in, an alleyway transformation project is underway, and the historic downtown district is being revitalized through public–private partnerships. James is well built for public service, and he loves making a difference in his local community. Still, that hardly means his work is not a struggle. It is a demanding job that comes with days he wants to forget and days he never will.

The human resources executive

Leslie leads the human resources department for a major Midwestern food service distributor—a position she has held for the past twenty-seven years. Her long tenure is even more remarkable considering that she landed the vice-president position after only a year at the company and without ever finishing college.

Her office is like many others. It has an executive suite and other offices organized by department. There is a break room with vending machines. Leslie's days are filled with benefits meetings, disciplinary meetings, lawyers, budgets, and the like. At the office, she is known as a person of deep Christian faith. Her colleagues know her faith is important to her because she is not shy about sharing it with others. For a number of years, she even organized a women's Bible study over the lunch hour.

The human resources department takes responsibility for the organizational culture and ensures that the employees are taken care of. Leslie's faith gives her a sense of purpose that sustains her long career in a single position at the same company. Being in a position that puts people and their well-being first resonates with Leslie's faith commitments. Being clear about those commitments, however, has at times driven her peers in the executive suite away.

The operations manager

Sally is the operations manager for a large utility company. She has been in that role for eight years, but she has been at the company for thirteen years. Her career has taken her much further than she initially imagined. After high school, Sally completed a year-long business program before returning home to the farming community she grew up in and where she now lives with her husband David. She held a number of jobs before her children were born, but she eventually settled into a thirteen-year stint as an administrator at her local Lutheran church.

When the family finances got tough, Sally explored opportunities beyond the church job, and she found a great opportunity at the utility company. Her starting salary there was twice what she got at the church.

At the utility company, Sally took advantage of opportunity after opportunity, eventually landing a supervisor position. She is the kind of supervisor who makes sure once a year to jump in the utility truck for a ride-along. It is a small thing, but it lets those she supervises know that she understands their day-to-day work. She treats all her colleagues like family and that makes her work very meaningful.

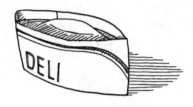

The meat department supervisor

John is a corporate supervisor for the grocery chain he started working at when he was just sixteen years old. School was not really John's thing, but the grocery store offered him an opportunity to learn a trade. As luck would have it, the family-owned company was also recruiting for its management program. Pretty soon, John was being mentored and groomed for a leadership role. At age twenty-three, he became an assistant manager, an uncommon achievement at the time.

Today, John supervises all the meat departments across the grocery store chain's 118 locations and eleven thousand employees. In a given week, he will drive eight hundred miles as he travels across the Midwest region. His day is filled with meetings and visiting stores. And while those things are important, John gets most excited these days about identifying younger employees who might be ready to take the next step in their careers.

Decades ago, John was mentored by others, and now he has the chance to do the same. John gets excited about this because he gets to take an interest in his employees, their families, and their lives outside of work. Mentoring makes his work much more than just a job.

The banker

Mitch is one of thirty regional presidents at one of the five largest banks in the United States, with seventy thousand employees. He attended a church-affiliated liberal arts college, where he played basketball. Originally, he wanted to become a doctor, but graduated college with a degree in math and without a clear sense of where his career would take him.

His career in the financial industry began shortly after he became the first from his family to graduate college. He worked for a few smaller banks, and eventually the bank where he worked was acquired by the national bank he now works for. Early on, Mitch helped grow the bank's business by providing lending services to car dealers. At this point in his career, much of his work has as much to do with people and team building as it does with loan applications and balance sheets.

As a banker, Mitch's work provides him with a generous salary, benefits, and the chance to play a meaningful role developing new managers at the bank. It also provides him with the flexibility to be involved in his local community, which the bank also regularly invests in. Mitch has a great job by nearly every measure, but for all the time that he spends investing in others, there are few—and often none—who can similarly invest in him.

Work in Classrooms and Clinics

While some professions may be difficult to imagine as callings, others are simply assumed to be. The so-called helping professions are among those that we often take for granted. Certainly, those who work as educators and healthcare providers have some kind of intrinsic motivation to dedicate their lives to serving others. The very nature of these jobs seems to make them good candidates for work as vocation.

It is certainly the case that many who work in classrooms and clinics chose these professions because they wanted to help and serve others. Below you will meet a few workers who tell stories just like that. In fact, even those who do not necessarily view their work in education and healthcare as a calling are often very selfless and caring people. But intent alone is not enough at work. Instead, the reality we find on the ground is that work in education and healthcare is profoundly shaped by the political and social realities of our divided American society. Often their work is misunderstood, and it is extraordinarily difficult to fully appreciate something you don't understand.

The teacher trainer

Valerie is a veteran educator who currently works as a teacher trainer in a fairly affluent suburban public school district.

Before this, she served in a post-secondary program focused on trades (similar to a community college), and before that she served in an under-resourced district. At this point, she has seen it all.

Prior to her career in education, Valerie spent a decade in a hospital purchasing department. When she was in the classroom, she brought a real-world sensibility to her teaching. These days, however, she does not spend any time in a classroom of her own. Instead, as a teacher trainer, she accompanies new teachers as they find their way into the field. Early on in her current district, Valerie got involved in the teacher's association. This often put her in the middle of conflicts between fellow teachers and school administrators.

Valerie embodies much of what we say we value about educators: she is talented, no-nonsense, and she would do anything for her students and her colleagues. But the story she tells about public education today is a complicated one. She tells a story about a broken educational system with little hope on the horizon.

The pharmacist

For the past thirty-four years, Jennifer has worked as a pharmacist at a medical network that was originally founded by an order of

Catholic nuns. Today, that network is one of the largest healthcare providers in the area.

Jennifer's mother was a nurse, so she understood the value of a career in medicine. She also knew there was no way she could ever be a nurse. Pharmacy, however, proved to require just the right mix of scientific knowledge and care for others—a perfect fit for her. At the pharmacy, Jennifer and her technicians will process hundreds of prescriptions every day. Every day, she faces a surprising number of challenges: Why has this patient come in for a refill too early? Is it a controlled substance they should be worried about, or is it an elderly patient who has the date wrong? And why hasn't this other patient picked up their refill? Are they okay? Why did another patient's doctor prescribe a medicine that can be dangerous when combined with the patient's medication from an unrelated condition? Might another doctor be willing to prescribe a different medication for this patient—one that the patient's insurance will actually cover? Despite this, Jennifer loves her job. She says she could do it until the day she dies.

The chiropractor

Laura is a chiropractor with her own private practice outside a large city. It is a small practice with just one other employee: an office assistant. Laura's assistant takes care of most things so that she can just focus on her patients. The work itself, as she describes it, is literally healing with her hands. Each patient is different, and it is her job to find the right combination of techniques and advice to help her patients.

Laura was introduced to chiropractic care when her family became converts. Her father was a long-haul truck driver who often had back problems. After he experienced its benefits, her mother also went, and it helped her chronic headaches—which Laura also suffered from. Soon they were all receiving treatment.

After college, she completed a program at a nearby chiropractic college, but the start of her practice was delayed until she found herself a single mother in need of some way to support herself. These days, she has remarried and the most important thing to her is being a mother, so she only works two days a week at the clinic. The other three she is at home to see the kids off to school and to be there when they get home.

The teacher turned real estate agent

For twenty-five years, Caroline taught physical education in the public schools of her suburban community. It was her own P.E. teacher who had been a mother figure to her during a tough childhood and who had inspired her to become a teacher.

Caroline was in her forties when her father died, and she began to wonder what else she might want to do with her life. Her dad had always wanted to get his real estate license, but he never did. By then, she and her husband had already flipped a few houses. She went for it, got her license, and for a while worked real estate part time before retiring from teaching to pursue it full time.

Caroline never really felt like teaching was a calling. Instead, she felt like being a mother was her calling in life. Her own childhood taught her the importance of a safe and stable home—something that is very important to her and her family. In a way, her work as a real estate agent is an extension of her belief that we all deserve a comfortable and safe home.

Work in Fields and Shops

On the surface, the kind of work that happens in the fields and in shops may seem to hearken back to a time before work was transformed by industrialization. So much of this work is still manual labor and the kind of work that is done by hand. Something about it seems simpler, less tainted by capitalism, globalization, or automated technology. We often think about this kind of work as somehow more honest than other kinds of work today.

There is no doubt that the workers who farm the fields and craft their handiwork in shops often think of their work more as a way of life than a job. Still, even these jobs have not escaped the ways the past two hundred years have fundamentally changed our work. Even a generation ago, many farmers grew crops to feed livestock, and then marketed the livestock at auction nearby. Today, farmers must constantly monitor the foreign market demand for their field corn and soybeans. And similar points could be made about nearly every tradecraft because supply chains today are all globally distributed. These realities came to the foreground with greater clarity during the coronavirus pandemic. Below you will meet some of those who work in fields and shops.

The farmer

David is a farmer who runs an eighteen-hundred-acre operation in the rural community in which he was born and raised. His brother-in-law is his business partner in the operation, and for years he also ran a seed business, which he recently sold to his son.

He always knew he would end up farming. It was a good thing, too, since none of his siblings had any interest in it. In the final years of the Vietnam War, David was called up for military service. After he completed his service, David returned home to farm. But those early years were difficult and soon he had to sell his farm. He spent a miserable year in the town's meat packing plant before he found a way back into farming, where he has been ever since.

During planting and harvest seasons, David, his brother-in-law, and his son will start the day over a pot of coffee, talking about sports. They talk about yesterday's work and what still has to be done before heading out. Once they do, they will not see each other again until the next morning. For David, there is little distinction between being a farmer and being a person of faith. To farm is to have faith because once the seed is in the ground, there is little else to do. "Well, everything is in God's hands now."

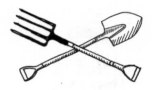

The farmer and bus driver

Karl farms the same land he purchased from his grandfather, which he hopes he will one day be able to sell to his son when he takes over. Like most farmers, his day begins before sunrise, but unlike other farmers, the first thing he drives each day is a school bus. He started this side job when cash was short on the farm, but it brings him so much joy that he has been doing it for twenty-four years now.

After the bus route, he heads to the livestock barns, where he lays down the remaining cornstarch from last year's harvest so that the cattle will be as comfortable as possible. In the afternoon, he picks up the hay bales he made the day before. Some evenings he volunteers as a lay minister, visiting others from the church he attends. Other nights he is on babysitting duty, helping his son navigate a difficult custody arrangement, which is critical if his son is ever going to be able to take over the farm.

Like many other farmers, Karl views his work as a calling. What is, perhaps, more surprising is that he also views his side job as a bus driver this way.

The hairdresser

Mary is a hairdresser in a rural community. At one point, she owned her own salon, but after she injured her wrist in a car accident, she could only work part time, so she sold it. Growing up, Mary had always wanted to be an architect. After graduating high school, she went to a large state college to pursue that dream. But her college town was very different from what she was used to. After just one semester, she returned home.

Her days at the salon are as you might expect. They are filled with clients coming in—some who have appointments and others who walk in. Some just want a trim, while others want the works. Work is usually accompanied by a bit of small talk and maybe even some town gossip, but sometimes it can be quiet too.

Mary is very gifted at what she does. She learned her craft from her grandmother. Other hairdressers may have some sense of calling to their work, but not Mary. For her, cutting hair simply provides a stable income. There will always be people who need their hair cut, so there will always be work as a hairdresser. It's just a job for her, but it's definitely not her dream job.

The farmer and small business owner

Sam is a farmer in a rural community where he was born and raised. He also owns several trucks that support local agricultural operations, a repair shop, and the town's bowling alley.

During the harvest, his days look like those of every other farmer. He is up by 5:00 a.m. and out in the field for fifteen hours or however long it takes to get the day's work done. Lately, he has been giving a hand to his son who is in his forties and trying to get into farming.

Once the harvest is over, the trucking operation slows down, and work at the repair shop really picks up. Local farmers go into "repair mode" ahead of spring planting, which means Sam and his eight employees at the shop will have plenty to do. They will start early, but by 4:30 p.m., you will find them gathered around a table. The refrigerator is always stocked, and the conversation is lively. Lately, politics keeps coming up. Sometimes he stops by on Sunday to find the whole crew there. "They've got their own church service going on there!"

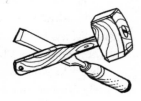

The casket maker

Ben spent most of his working life in sales, but today he works alongside the brothers of a Catholic monastery who own and operate a casket-making operation to support their ministry. He helps in the shop, making caskets, giving tours, and delivering the caskets to funeral homes.

If he does not have a tour to give, Ben spends a lot of time alone. He might be in the back of the shop preparing some part of a casket. Or he could be making a delivery to a funeral home hours away. Whenever he is alone, he likes to spend time reflecting on his relationship with God. Although he is not Catholic, faith is a very important part of Ben's life, and he really values working at a place where he can openly express that.

Even though his day starts early, Ben does not mind because this is the best job he's ever had. He finds his work with the brothers very satisfying, even if the pay could be a little better.

***

Already these brief introductions to the workers you will encounter throughout this book demonstrate the diversity present in today's world of work. Some of the work we will encounter in the following pages has deep roots in the history of work described earlier. Other kinds of work more readily reflect the significant ways work changed after the Industrial Revolution. One constant, however, is the sheer amount of time we spend doing our work. That time alone raises questions about the meaning and purpose of work today. The focus throughout this book is on how everyday workers themselves make meaning, but before we dive into these stories, it will be helpful to consider the primary story the church and its theology tells about the meaning of our working lives. It is to that story that we now turn.

2

Improvising with Vocation

> We must not, like these asses, ask the Latin letters how we are to speak German; but we must ask the mother in the home, the children on the street, the common man in the marketplace about this, and look them in the mouth to see how to speak, and afterwards do our translation.
>
> —Martin Luther, *On Translation*

What does the world of work have to do with Christian faith? In this chapter, we will explore that very question. While the church and its theology might intersect with our working lives in a number of ways, the most significant intersection can be found in the theology of vocation—a theological development that has its roots in the time of the Reformation and the writings of Martin Luther. Since then, thinking about work as a vocation or a "calling" has been the most common way Protestant churches have thought about the meaning of our working lives.

In recent decades, a few theologians (this one included!) have raised serious questions about our theologies of vocation. What's most important for our purposes is simply that we understand how we got here. How did the Protestant theology of vocation develop and how is it used today in the lives of ordinary people of faith?

But first, it is important to remember that whether we are thinking about the writings of Martin Luther in the sixteenth century or our working lives today, theology cares about our working lives because a key claim of the Christian faith is that God is *at work* in the world. So if God is at work and our lives are fundamentally shaped by the work we do—both paid and unpaid—then the big question is this: *What is the relationship between God's work and ours?* This is not an easy question, and how theology has tried to address this question has changed over time. As we turn now to the historical development of Luther's theology of vocation and its practical role in working lives today, keep that big question in mind.

The Vocational Script

Today, the word *vocation* carries both religious and non-religious connotations. On the one hand, we use the word to refer to those professions we call trades, such as when we use phrases like "vocational training" or "vocational school." On the other hand, some continue to use vocation synonymously with the notion of being called to a particular kind of work. This latter use echoes an older and more explicitly religious use of the term. At the time of the Protestant Reformation, Martin Luther developed a theology of vocation that was quite different from the one he inherited as a sixteenth-century monk.

Back then, vocation referred to the special calling of priests and those belonging to religious orders. Underwriting this usage was a way of dividing the world into sacred and secular realms. The former was thought to be the sphere of God's work, while the latter was basically bad. If one wanted to live a truly Christian life, you had to fully dedicate yourself to the work of the church. These religious "elites" were the ones who had callings, and they practiced a kind of virtuoso Christianity.

To get a sense of just how far this sense of vocation could go, consider the case of Walter of Chaumont, a French man living in the twelfth century. He was inspired by the examples of others in the Cistercian Order, and he thought perhaps he should join the monastery at Clairvaux. There was only one problem: his mother was sick and needed him to take care of her. Torn between joining the monastery and continuing to take care of his mother, he wrote a letter seeking the advice of the abbot, Bernard of Clairvaux. Here's a brief excerpt from the reply Walter received from Bernard: "Your mother's wish, being contrary to your salvation, is equally so to her own. Choose, therefore, of these two alternatives which you will: either, that is, to secure the wish of one or the salvation of both. But if you love her so much, have the courage to leave her for her sake, lest if you leave Christ to remain with her, she also will perish on your account."[1]

Those are some harsh words, and it's tempting to dismiss them as the words of a self-serving religious leader out of touch with the needs of the real world. But, in his words we can also see this stark division between the sacred world where vocations were divinely mandated, and the secular world where a working life had very little to do with God's work in the world. This is an important context for understanding why Luther felt compelled to reject this version of vocation.

Simply put: Luther listened to the way vocation was being used in his day and realized that limiting vocational calling to clergy and other virtuoso religious elites did little for ordinary people of faith trying to make sense of their everyday existence. Luther improvised with the vocational theology of his day and transformed it into a way of talking theologically about what one Luther scholar called "the whole theatre of personal, communal, and historical relationships in which one lives."[2] Everyone had not just one, but many vocations because all Christians are called to love and serve our neighbors—all those people we encounter in the midst of our daily lives.

Across Luther's writings we find this turn to daily life. For example, when Luther interprets "give us this day our daily bread" in the Lord's Prayer, he says this has to do with much more than

---

1 William Placher, *Callings: Twenty Centuries of Christian Wisdom on Vocation* (Grand Rapids, MI: Eerdmans Publishing, 2005), 134–135.
2 Marc Kolden, "Luther on Vocation," *Word and World* 3, no. 4 (1983), 384.

just our daily sustenance; it includes food, shelter, and health, but those forces that shape them too. That means every aspect of our home, civic, and political life are also part of our daily bread.[3] Another example can be found in the preface of Luther's German translation of the Bible. There, Luther makes a point about the work of translation that reflects his way of doing theology. He insisted on listening to the language and experiences of ordinary people, and only then turning to the work of interpretation and theology.[4]

As the Protestant Reformation spread, so did its ideas and among them was this more improvisational version of vocation. In Geneva, John Calvin incorporated much of Luther's insights, especially the idea that vocation belonged to everyone, and not just some class of spiritual elites. Calvin also affirmed that much of what might be thought of as "secular work" could serve God's purposes. But he elaborated Luther's thinking in two important ways.

First, Calvin observed that we are not all born with the same talents and abilities. From that he concludes that it's not just individuals who have a vocation, but entire societies. And second, God's purposes should be carried out not just by individuals living into their callings, but by a divinely ordered society working together collectively.[5] Within both the Lutheran and the Reformed theologies, vocation was a calling for everyday Christians to faithfully engage the world around them. Before the Reformation, those with vocations seemed removed from the secular world;

---

3 Kathryn Kleinhans, "The Work of a Christian: Vocation in Lutheran Perspective," *Word and World* 25, no. 4 (Fall 2005), 398.

4 Martin Luther, "On Translating: An Open Letter, 1530," in vol. 35, *Luther's Works*, American ed. E. Theodore Bachmann ed. (Philadelphia: Fortress, 1960), 189.

5 Lee Hardy, *The Fabric of this World: Inquiries in Calling, Career Choice, and the Design of Human Work* (Grand Rapids, MI: Eerdmans, 1990), 60–67.

now vocation was the very vehicle for God's redemptive work in the world.

In Luther's original thinking, we are called to work in particular "stations," or occupations. All stations had the potential to be vocations. But because medieval society did not include a whole lot of social mobility, Luther's vocational theology seemed to justify the fact that some were born into wealth or privilege, while others were born to be peasants. Since God worked through all stations, there was no reason to aspire toward better work and, therefore, a better life. Calvin's emphasis on abilities and talents put the emphasis less on the work itself and instead on how one did the work. This flexibility allowed the Reformed theology of vocation to address social injustices more adequately and challenge the static social world of medieval Europe.

From our brief history of the world of work, you will recall that significant historical developments took place between the eighteenth and twentieth centuries. Surprisingly, the same cannot really be said for the Protestant theologies of vocation. Twentieth-century theologians have sought to recover a Lutheran theology of vocation as a way of making sense of the profound social changes that emerged at the beginning of the century. The most well-known of these is Swedish theologian Gustaf Wingren, whose seminal work called *Luther on Vocation* set the stage for generations of vocational renewal.

The oldest of five children, Wingren was born in 1910 to a working-class family. His father worked at a tannery near Valdemarsvik, and Wingren would have followed in his father's footsteps and taken up the family trade were it not for a severely deformed hand. His physical disability, however, earned him additional time in school, and he became the first in his family to attend university. At the University of Lund, Wingren would eventually earn his doctorate and join the faculty there. He entered the theological scene during a time historians call the "Swedish Luther Renaissance"—a movement that sought to recenter the writings of Martin Luther in Lutheranism. Wingren's turn to vocation was one of many efforts to reclaim the significance of Luther's theology for modern life.

Luther on Vocation[6] is a whirlwind exploration of Luther's writings, which emphasizes two features of Luther's improvisation of vocation. First, vocation is "particular," meaning that while all Christians share a "general" call to be disciples of Christ in the world, we always do so in a particular time and place. We are not called to be all things to all people; instead, we live out our callings in different ways in different times and among different people. In Wingren's reading, Luther encourages us to take these differences into account and to discover for ourselves where and to whom we are called.[7] Second, vocation is always "public" in the sense that it is always, in the first place, about one's neighbors. That is, vocation is just a fancy word for all the ways we might love and serve others. From a Lutheran perspective, it is precisely because we understand salvation as a gift and there is nothing more for us to do to earn it, that we are freed to fully engage with the world. In a memorable line from Wingren, he summarizes Luther in this way: "God does not need our good works, but our neighbor does."[8]

Wingren and generations of theologians that followed began including vocation as one of the most significant developments of the Protestant Reformation. Within these efforts, however, was an assumption that most ordinary people of faith experienced a basic kind of meaninglessness. That's because when theologians look at society today, they often see a way of life that is fragmented and compartmentalized. It is meaningless because there is nothing to integrate the various parts of our everyday life—our family life, our work life, our church life, our public life, and so on—into a coherent whole. Vocation, these theologians would say, is relevant

---

6 Gustaf Wingren, *Luther on Vocation*. (Eugene, OR: Wipf and Stock, reprinted 2004).

7 Wingren, *Luther on Vocation*, 1–18.

8 Wingren, *Luther on Vocation*, 10.

because it offers us a way of integrating our lives around our particular calling.

I call this way of thinking about vocation a "script" because that is the way many theologians today imagine theology influencing everyday life. Think for a moment about the way scripts work in other contexts. They are written out ahead of time and given to actors, so they know what to say and what to do once they get on stage. Scripts are like blueprints; they are worked out ahead of time and they are meant to be followed by others as closely as possible. That is, they are *prescriptive*.

At its best, the vocational script offers ordinary Christians a way of interpreting what they encounter in the theatre of their everyday lives. In this way, the vocational script shares with Luther a concern for daily living. It also shares with Luther two additional convictions. It shares his conviction that there is a relationship between God's work and ours and it shares his conviction that there are no virtuoso religious elites. No matter what shape our everyday lives take, some callings are not more important or more spiritual than others.

There is no doubt that many ordinary Christians have found the vocational script to be a meaningful way to think about their life. This way of thinking about the meaning of work is common among professions such as teachers, doctors, and public service. But it is by no means limited to helping professions and service-oriented careers. The vocational script can be applied to nearly any job where the worker feels especially suited for it, as if they were meant to do it. The script is a powerful way of expressing a passion or sense of purpose at work, so much so that while Christians use the script to link work and faith, the term *vocation* is just as easily found in entirely secular settings.

Going Off Script

When I set out to interview workers from a variety of professions, I expected to find that some thought about their work as a calling and had adopted this vocational script. I also expected that others probably wouldn't think of their work this way. What I didn't expect to discover is just how complicated it can be to actually practice vocation in today's world of work. I couldn't have anticipated the conditions that would cause some to adopt the vocational script while others went off script.

As it turns out, the vocational script is just one of many stories ordinary workers tell themselves and others about the meaning of their work. Those theologians who assumed that modern life was void of meaning were wrong! The problem is not that there is a lack of meaning, it's that there is a surplus of meanings. Our families of origin teach us about the meaning and purpose of work, our schooling further teaches us things about our work, and workplaces themselves have explicit ways of narrating why they do what they do. In fact, we can think of all these contributions as a repertoire, or a collection of narratives that we can draw on when telling ourselves and others about the meaning of our work. If you ask someone what their work means to them, they are likely to rehearse a story—or perhaps several stories—from that repertoire. Depending on the situation and who is doing the asking, that story may change. That's because our working lives don't mean just one thing to us.

Actually, it's even more complicated than that because the meaning of our working lives can change over time. How we think about our work can change as our interests change or as we gain experience. It can change if we start families and develop new priorities concerning our time and resources. Organizations and professions also change, and what might have been a good fit at one point is suddenly a very bad one. Even relatively minor changes, such as getting a new boss, can dramatically change whether one has a good job or a bad one.

Change is the one thing we can count on when it comes to our working lives, and that's the problem with the vocational script. The problem with scripts is that they are, by definition, intended to sort out the meaning and direction of a story beforehand. Scripts have the beginning, middle, and end of a story already in view. The problem is that is not how our everyday lives work in the modern world.

Since at least the early twentieth century, theologians and other religious leaders have used our theologies of vocation in a prescriptive way. While Luther pointed to the *potential* of all work to be a calling, theologians and religious leaders today often talk and write about vocation in a way that suggests all workers *should* see their work as a calling. We've turned the vocational script into our prescription for meaning-making.

To get a sense of what I mean, consider this. The year was 1925 in Stockholm, Sweden at an early conference of the ecumenical movement; a group of church leaders and theologians had gathered to discuss the theme "Faith and Work." There were many at the conference who felt strongly that a renewed theology of vocation would help ordinary Christians meet the challenges and ethical demands of work in the early twentieth century. The more they talked to one another, however, the wider the gap between theology and everyday life seemed. At one point, a Swedish bishop and former professor said:

> Very often when I have been talking to a businessman, a great employer and a leader of men, about these and similar questions, I have left him with a sense of humiliation. I used to think that I as a professor of ethics should be able to tell him his duty and to find fault with him. But as soon as such men started to speak about their practical difficulties and their experiences, and to ask me in return how I would have acted in such and such circumstances, I had to admit myself unable to answer. I have very often been able to find that they had made far more serious attempts to solve the ethical questions than I had imagined. And I have had to admit that I simplified matters too much

and that the problems which I look upon as very simple in reality consisted of a number of technical questions. The man with whom I used to debate these things had like myself felt the dualism between the ethical and the technical points of view very painfully. And thus, we began, instead of disputing about different points of view, to try to penetrate deeper and more comprehensively into the problem. Thereby we were brought to realize still more clearly how impossible it is to dictate a ready solution to such a complicated economic social problem.[9]

The irony is that this admission can be found in between overly romanticized speeches about recovering vocation from the theological treasure chest of the Reformation. This Swedish bishop had discovered what I did: that the demands of work today don't always fit neatly into some predetermined script.

Before diving more deeply into this idea of going "off script," it is important to say something about the role of stories and how stories themselves are related to meaning-making. Stories are, as one of my teachers used to say, "the coins of the realm," or the currency for making sense of the world around us. Through storytelling, our personal experiences can be shared with others. If you're looking for the meaning of our everyday lives, you will find it in the stories people tell.

Of course, not all stories are the same. Some stories, such as personal ones about our everyday lives, are idiosyncratic. These stories point toward the uniqueness and individuality of our lives. These stories are first lived and then told in episodes or even shorter fragments. An example of this kind of story might go like this:

---

9   George K. A. Bell, ed., *The Stockholm Conference 1925: The Official Report of the Universal Christian Conference on Life and Work held in Stockholm, 19–30 August, 1925* (London: Oxford University Press, 1926), 195.

The other day I was in a meeting, and someone said something so ridiculous that I had to say something. After two years, I still feel like the new guy, so I try to mostly listen in these meetings. But I knew what this guy was saying was wrong, and I was sure others did too. So I raised my hand and pushed back . . . hard. I was relieved to see so many others nodding their heads as I spoke. I was finally starting to find my voice among my colleagues.

I call very brief personal stories like these *narrative fragments*. They don't tell all the details, but they share enough to get a sense of what happened and why it was significant. I call personal stories with more detail and context *narrative episodes*. These kinds of fragments and episodes make up a large number of the stories that my interviewees shared with me, and they are common in our everyday discourse. As time goes by, we accumulate more and more of these in our repertoires of meaning.

Another kind of story we might find in those repertoires I call *value narratives*. These are stories we learn from our families, from schooling, or even at the workplace. Value narratives make claims about the character of this or that kind of work. These stories often appear in conversations we share with others who become important characters in our lives. But they can also appear in the myriad of ways workplaces themselves justify their existence. Take, for example, the following selection of corporate mission statements:

We're in business to save our home planet.
To inspire healthier communities by connecting people to real food.
To create a better everyday life for the many people.

Even these singular statements tell a story about the purpose and meaning of work. If you work at one of these companies—in order of appearance, Patagonia, Sweetgreen, or IKEA—the value narrative here suggests that you are contributing to a lofty and unquestionably positive end goal.

There is one more kind of story that you will find in the pages that follow, which I call *metanarratives*, a term that has been used by scholars in a whole host of ways. For our purposes, what is important about these stories is that they are rooted in culture and history; because of this, they are stories shared in common among entire groups of people. Perhaps the best-known example of a metanarrative about work in the United States is the narrative we call "the American Dream." That story basically goes like this: *Success in American society is available to anyone, regardless of where they were born and regardless of their past or current circumstances. In this country, what matters is our talents and abilities. With enough hard work, upward mobility and success are available to everyone.*

What makes this metanarrative interesting is that it doesn't take much to demonstrate that this is a story we tell about the way we *want* our country to be. It certainly isn't a story that is grounded in the actual lived experiences of all or even most Americans. The hard truth is that the American Dream is only true for a relatively small group of people.

Many of us were born into families that could pass on significant generational wealth. And many of us were not born into families like that.

Many of us were born into families that could provide us with the kind of education and support that make economic success and family stability probable. And many of us were not born into families like that either.

Many of us were lucky. We were at the right place at the right time, and that led to success for us and for our families. And many of us just were not that lucky.

Many of us enjoy or desire all the things that the American Dream promises—steady employment, ample savings for retirement, and home ownership—especially a big house in the suburbs near great schools for the kids with everything you need in a short driving distance. And many of us have never wanted any of that anyway.

What is interesting is that despite these complexities and the growing number of Americans for whom this story has never made much sense, we continue to tell this story. It is embedded in our national consciousness. It is passed on from generation to generation through casual conversation, through advertising, and in popular culture. We all know this story, whether or not it applies to us. That's what makes this kind of story so powerful. And it's what makes it so difficult to change.

If you ask ordinary people to tell you about their lives and how they find meaning in their day-to-day lives, you're likely to hear all three of these kinds of stories: narrative fragments or episodes, value narratives, and metanarratives. Most of us have a good number of each in those repertoires we carry with us.

I mentioned above that the problem with scripts is that they are by nature prescriptive, and that doesn't exactly match the realities of our everyday lives. This raises important questions about what it looks like when we find ourselves having to go "off script."

What if the vocational script has never really described how I understand my work? Or, what about instances when the vocational script stops working because the conditions at work change and it no longer seems to be a calling?

The stories and scripts we use to tell ourselves and others about the meaning of our work have a pragmatic dimension to them. What I mean by that is that these stories themselves have work to do. The stories are *at work* because they help us pull together what otherwise seems random, disconnected, or fragmented. They answer basic existential questions such as: *Why am I working so hard for this? What is all of this for? Is all this time and energy worth it?*

Borrowing a clever phrase from social theorist Peter Berger, I call this pragmatic dimension of our everyday storytelling its "plausibility structures."[10] Berger was writing about the relationship between religion and modern society when he coined this phrase. He was talking about the way religion made sense of the world around us. If religion was to continue, what it offered had to plausibly help ordinary people make sense of their experiences of the world. In a narrower sense, the stories we tell ourselves and others about the meaning of our work must also match our actual experiences at work.

It's hard to tell yourself and others that you get to go to work every day and change the world if you spend most of your time at work in pointless meetings or filling out redundant paperwork. At some point, that's not a plausible story, and many find that there's usually two ways out of such a bind: you can either tell a different story or live your way into a new story.

When the stories we tell are no longer plausible, it's time to improvise. There are no scripts, of course, for improvisation. Instead, like jazz musicians who riff through their solos, improvising with vocation requires that we draw on our faith, what we know about our work, our sense of purpose in the world beyond work, and past experiences to forge a new story. The result is just as meaningful as scripts, but what emerges in such improvised stories is a very different kind of meaning-making.

In the end, the stories that stayed with me long after my interviewees shared them with me were those improvised ones. They were the grittier stories: stories of work's daily grind, stories of disappointment or failure, crucible episodes that would forever alter what followed, such as second careers or midlife crises. So many of these stories included situations that simply couldn't have been anticipated. I learned that it was much more difficult to predict the ways people found meaning in their work, but I

---

10 Peter L. Berger, *The Sacred Canopy: Elements of A Sociological Theory of Religion* (New York: Anchor Books, 1967), 45.

grew to prefer these improvised stories with all their twists and turns over the prescriptive vocational script.

It was an awkward revelation for me, the theologian. I had thought the task in front of me was to find new ways to talk about and teach our classical theological insights, such as vocation. I thought I had what my interviewees needed. I was wrong. As it turns out, what this theologian needed was to be introduced to a new kind of source material for doing theology. I found that in these improvised stories about ordinary working lives today. There is still much work to do as I relearn what it looks like to do theology beginning not with scripts, but with improvised stories from everyday lives. I will have to learn for myself how to improvise, but that is a story yet to be written. In the meantime, I want to share with you twenty six stories from my interviewees. I'll introduce each one by connecting it to my own story, and I hope you will do the same.

3

Seeds

Some of the most powerful stories are *origin* stories. By telling the story of our work "from the beginning," we catch a glimpse of how far we have come and where things may be headed. Sometimes the meaning of our working lives is even foreshadowed in these early episodes. At other times, our stories take surprising turns that were anything but self-evident when we began this journey.

Perhaps one of the most persistent myths about work today is that we can be anything we want to be. Even if that were potentially true, it does not reflect how our everyday lives actually unfold. In reality, it's as if we have walked onto a stage of a theatrical production already in its second or third act. There are histories in-play—and here I mean small histories such as those from our families of origin but also larger stories such as those that shape American society. These histories shape the possibilities and limits of our own trajectories. Where we begin and the people we meet along the way play key roles in the stories of our working lives.

As we grow up, there are also other narratives at work. Some of these narratives make claims about what counts as "good work," who should do certain kinds of work, and what matters most about our working lives. These powerful scripts shape how our working lives unfold just as much, if not more, than what we *want* to do.

The stories that follow make this much abundantly clear: *just as important as what we do is how we got there.* In the pages that follow, you will hear stories of work that seems inevitable, pre-ordained almost. You will find stories that seem to have unfolded completely by chance. You will meet workers whose possibilities seem limited only by their imaginations and others who seem to have been dealt a bad hand. These stories paint a complicated picture—one that defies any effort to reduce the meaning of work to a single story or script.

What you are about to read is kind of a mess. The origin stories in this first section reveal that our working lives are like the parable that Jesus tells about the Sower. Some of the seeds fall on good soil, others on rocky soil, and others never take root. When Jesus tells this parable, he seems to be suggesting that despite the conditions "on the ground," the Sower continues to tend to the seed. Likewise, the collective invitation of the stories in this section is to listen for echoes of the Sower's care and provision despite the terrain.

"Born to Farm"

Perhaps I should begin with a confession. *I have a hard time imagining not being a theologian.* I was in my mid-20s before I even thought about being a professional theologian. But now it is such a central part of who I am that I have a hard time imagining being anything else. While being a theologian is a weird job, it shares with other professions a way of getting into your very bones. I cannot imagine there are many theologians out there who stop being a theologian when they go home for the day. Being a theologian is not just a job; it's an identity. It becomes a defining part of how you understand yourself, how you understand others, and how you understand the world. I suppose that is why I have a hard time imagining not being a theologian. If I were to stop being a theologian, I would have to rethink everything.

And I would rather not rethink *everything*.

***

At the time of the Reformation, social mobility was virtually unheard of. If you happened to be born the son or daughter of a craftsman, you were quite likely to become a craftsman or marry one. Similarly, if you were born into wealth, you would likely continue to live a life of luxury. These static social realities were a part of what Martin Luther had in mind when he wrote about our "stations" in life. Stations are, well, *stationary*.

With Industrialization and the rise of modern capitalism came the middle class and many more opportunities to transcend the economic conditions and social stratum we are born into. In his writings on vocation, Luther is trying to assure ordinary Christians that they could serve God even in their so-called "lower" stations. Modern readers of Luther ought to question the way his writings seem to underwrite these static social orders—as if they were ordained by God. Today, social mobility is taken for granted as part of American life. It is the very foundation of that story we tell called "the American Dream."

It's worth noting that Luther's notion of vocation within one's station of life and the American Dream are at polar odds with each other. Both are narratives about the meaning of our working lives, but they are very different narratives with very different assumptions. What both the vocational script and the American Dream share, however, is a one-size-fits-all approach to the meaning of our work. For Luther, God is at work in every station, so there is no need to leave or look beyond one's station in life. For the American Dream, God is at work in the opportunities to transcend one's station.

Neither of these two narratives seem to account for the wide range of ways that ordinary people tell the story of their working lives. When listening to the stories of ordinary workers, I was surprised by the wide range of origin stories, and it only makes sense to begin with the kind of origin story that suggests that perhaps some of us are born to do this or that job.

***

"Well, I am a farmer, and I guess I got into that line of work because I was born and raised a farmer."

That is how David introduced himself to me a few years ago. He grew up in a small agricultural community in the Midwest. As David put it:

Everything back then was connected with agriculture. I mean, you either milked the cows or you knew the guy that hauled the milk. You either fed the pigs, or you knew the guy that slaughtered the pigs. And you knew the guy at the co-op, the guy that you bought the feed from. Back then, everybody I knew was connected to what we all did for our job.

David's father was a farmer as was his grandfather before him. One of four boys growing up, David is the only one still behind a tractor, though two of his brothers work for a major farm equipment retailer. His brother-in-law (also a farmer) is also his business partner. David recently sold his seed operation to his son and, if all goes well, his son will eventually take over the farming operation.

Of all the workers I interviewed, the farmers were among the clearest about the relationship between God's work and theirs. Here is what David told me when I asked about a time when he found his work particularly meaningful:

Almost every day. That's what makes a farmer a unique, or odd, fellow. I mean because it's the connection that you have with God. Because you take the New Testament, Jesus talks a lot about growing something. And that's what we do. When you can see it from that seed, and you see it all the way through until it's in the bed again. That's quite something.

When you see all of these things happening—what I deal with is seasonally. You plant that seed, you take care of that seed, and you harvest that seed. It's no different than a year out of our lives. It's the same thing. I don't see a lot of difference. And I cannot, I cannot imagine doing what I do without God. I mean, it's a direct link.

Whether he knows it or not, David's story reflects the way Luther might describe God at work within ordinary stations of life. There may be hints of the American Dream narrative in the way David describes his own work ethic and the success he has had, but it's pretty clear that he was not looking to transcend the hand he was dealt. Rather, he was trying to continue a long family legacy of farming—a legacy that has made its home on the same plot of land for generations.

***

David's story introduces perhaps the most important theological question about our contemporary working lives: *Do we choose our work? Or is our work part of some divine plan?*

Listening to his story, it is almost as if God had pre-ordained it from the very beginning. Perhaps David really was born and raised to farm. If this were the case for everyone, we would quickly dismiss it as a form of oppression—something out of the dystopian pages of Aldous Huxley's *Brave New World*. But David would not likely accept that assessment. He loves being a farmer. Farming has provided David a sense of purpose, the financial means to support his family, the freedom to volunteer in his community, and the opportunity to care for God's creation, which he clearly understands as an expression of his Christian faith.

But why is it that so few of us have David's clarity of purpose? Even though I can hardly imagine not being a theologian today, I don't think I was born for this. If I were born for one singular purpose in life, as David's story suggests, I must have missed the memo. What kind of God would craft some grand design and then fail to distribute the instructions to everyone involved? God as an incompetent career planner is not quite an image that resonates with me.

But there are, of course, further questions. If God does have the kind of plan that ascribes to each of us the perfect career, what about those who work in dehumanizing or dangerous conditions? What about those who are exploited for their labor? I cannot accept that those jobs are a part of God's plan. Neither am I willing to place the onus on the worker—as if God does have a plan but we all just need to get with the program. That cannot be right.

On the other hand, to say that our work is simply our choice does not seem to fit the lived experiences of workers like David either. That puts the agency squarely in his court and seems to discount the whole idea of "being born to farm." When David says he was born for this, he is pointing toward a sense of purpose that is beyond himself, beyond his own little world and the life he has made for himself.

David's story may raise this central theological question, but his story alone sure doesn't resolve it. Perhaps some more stories will point us toward some other possibilities.

"You're an Engineer"

It was my junior year of college, and I was on the phone with my mother. I told her I was changing majors and that I wanted to go to seminary after college.

"I've always known you'd be a pastor," she said in response. *Wait, what?*

I was very confused. First of all, it was not all that clear to me that I *would* be a pastor or that I would be a *good* one. In fact, other theology majors had joked that I would be the *worst* pastor—because I used too many four-letter words. Besides, I had only said I wanted to go to seminary. I had not said anything about the p-word. And second, if she had *always* known, why hadn't she said anything before now?

To be fair, my mother meant for her words to be encouraging. She had not intentionally withheld top secret divine knowledge from me. It just felt that way because before I had worked up the courage to tell her about my career change, I had really struggled with the decision.

What was I supposed to do with my life?

***

In recent years, no one has articulated the vocational script quite like Frederick Buechner. In his well-known book *Wishful Thinking*,

Buechner describes vocation as this: "The place God calls you is where your deep gladness and the world's deep hunger meet."[1]

I doubt Luther would agree with Buechner's seemingly singular fulcrum. Luther, after all, was clear that we are called to multiple vocations at once. Still, Buechner's description of vocation is certainly scripted. Notice the logic at work here. It is as if in God's grand design, God placed somewhere deep inside your inner being a gladness or a joy that is activated upon discovering some pressing need in the world. Where Luther and Buechner would likely agree is that God calls us to *particular* vocations.

This is one of the geniuses of Luther. The Medieval church had long taught that everyone has a *general* vocation: to become and be a Christian (and a good one at that!). What set clergy and other religious orders apart is that they also had a *particular* vocation: to serve God as priests, monks, and nuns. Luther's theology of vocation improvised with that original teaching and extended the possibility of a *particular* vocation to everyone. Not only does God call us to discipleship, but God also calls us to particular kinds of work. Buechner's formula is designed to help others discern or hear God's call on their lives.

Find that intersection of deep gladness and need, and there you will find God's voice.

***

It would be difficult to find someone clearer about their sense of calling to serve the needs of others than Jeff. When I met him, he was emphatic about this sense of calling. It was something his pastor had preached on regularly at church, and it was something he and his wife had repeated over and over to their children. When I heard Jeff tell the story about how he became a city planner in a

---

1 Frederick Buechner, *Wishful Thinking: A Theological ABC* (San Francisco: Harper San Francisco, 1993), 119.

large Midwestern town, it made sense why the vocational script had become such a good fit for him. The way Jeff tells it, he was hardwired to become an engineer from the very beginning:

> *Ever since I was a young kid, I was laser focused, I was going to be an engineer. And I had a grandmother that reinforced that. She kept saying, 'You're an engineer.' And she would give me stuff to fix and work on and take apart. And I did that. So now I, even to this day, I'm the guy that fixes stuff.*

Jeff was raised in a middle-class home where both parents worked. His father had once worked for a major computer company, but the stress and anxiety of that work drove him to a simpler way of life as a groundskeeper at a nearby national cemetery. His mother worked the night shift as a waitress. Jeff's grandmother stepped in when his working parents needed someone to look after him. This gave her plenty of chances to encourage Jeff.

Jeff's grandmother saw something in him that made her declare: *You're an engineer.* That three-word narrative took on a life of its own. When his grandmother gave him things to take apart, it was a chance for Jeff to embody the script laid out before him. He was living into the story his grandmother told him.

By the time he was headed to college to study engineering, it was as if his grandmother had spoken his destiny into existence. In the years that followed college, Jeff went to work for a private engineering firm. A few years into the job, he met his future wife on a blind date. After they married, Jeff took a job working for a county so that they could be closer to her family. Soon a baby was on the way too.

Six months into the new position, he was let go.

Newly unemployed and with a baby on the way, Jeff used the extra time to complete his civil engineer license and he threw himself into some of the latest design software. He lucked out.

The same company that created the software he was learning had an opening in a nearby town.

This time, the position was a much better fit.

Twelve years later, a former colleague called Jeff and asked him to come work for the city. He was doing well and wasn't really looking for a new job. Reluctantly, he interviewed anyway. Initially when they offered him the position, he declined.

Two days later, his phone rang again.

"We'd really like for you to come work for the city," his former colleague said.

"Okay, alright. Well, you'll have to give me three weeks' vacation, and this is where I want to start at for the salary," Jeff told him.

"Done."

It was a bit of a rocky start, but having spent the last fourteen years as the city's civil engineer, maybe, somehow, Jeff's grandmother was right. *Maybe he was destined for this work.*

***

I never asked Jeff whether or not his work was his "deep gladness," and it's difficult to say whether or not city planning is one of the world's "deep hungers." Perhaps Buechner's framework is a little dramatic.

Still, what does it mean that some people, like Jeff and David (the farmer), seem destined for their occupations, while others spend years trying to figure out what they are supposed to do in life?

My experience listening to stories of work makes it tempting to see God as some kind of vocational engineer who has a master plan, complete with *particular* vocations for each and every one of us. In some of the stories that follow, in hindsight, it can seem as if some working lives follow God's master plan as though our particular vocations are predestined from the beginning. But there will be other stories that resist that idea altogether. And this is one of the reasons why we need to learn to move beyond the vocational script. The script cannot account for many of the actual lives we lead.

Maybe we need a new way of thinking about Luther's notion of our *general* and *particular* vocations. Maybe it is not that God has some master plan: *this one will be a pastor and that one will be an engineer.* Rather than a prescription, perhaps our vocational theologies might simply describe how it is that God comes to us, not in some *general* way, but in the details —in our actual daily lives and among the people we actually meet there. Perhaps they can become a way of naming the *particular* ways God shows up as we all struggle to find our place in the world.

***

Dear Mom,

   I'm sorry, but I don't think I'm going to be a pastor when I grow up. In fact, it's much worse than that. I'm going to be a professional theologian.

Love,
Tim.

"My Dad Was a Salesman"

For the better part of my secondary education, I wanted to be a band director. In sixth grade I picked up the trombone for the first time, and from that point on, music played a defining role in my life. I may not have been that good early on, but by high school, I could really play. When I began telling people I was headed to college to study music, no one was surprised. Music had taught me valuable lessons: hard work, dedication, the pursuit of excellence, and music's powerful ability to express the human experience. I was excited about the possibility of passing on those lessons to other young people. I was confident this was my path.

***

What makes our work *good*?

One reason we tell stories about our working lives is to convince ourselves and others that we, indeed, do *good* work. Yet, "good" here is surprisingly amorphous and less certain than we might think. Sometimes it is the products or services our work provides. Those are good things, and so creating them, we say, is good. Sometimes "good" just means that going to work is tolerable or reasonably respectful. After all, some workplaces do not value their workers and others outright abuse them. Sometimes the compensation offered is sufficient enough to accept that the work itself is uninteresting or mundane or difficult.

Much of work, however, is not good at all. David Graeber, the late anthropologist, wrote that today's world of work is particularly *good* at creating "bullshit jobs."[2] He identified five types:

- *Flunky* jobs are those that exist only or primarily exist to make someone else look or feel important; they are unnecessary subordinates (e.g., doormen and receptionists).
- *Goons* are jobs that have an aggressive element, but crucially, who exist only because other people employ them (e.g., lobbyists and telemarketers).

---

2 David Graeber, *Bullshit Jobs: A Theory* (New York: Simon & Schuster, 2018).

- *Duct tapers* are jobs that exist only because of a glitch or fault in the organization; [they are there] to solve a problem that ought not exist (e.g., some computer programmers and data specialists).
- *Box tickers* exist only or primarily to allow an organization to be able to claim it is doing something that, in fact, it is not doing (e.g., compliance offices and quality control officers).
- *Taskmasters* assign work to others [when] they believe that were not there, underlings would be perfectly capable of carrying on by themselves; they are unnecessary superiors (e.g., middle managers).[3]

Of course, when asked as a young child, "What do you want to be when you grow up?" no one says, "I'd like to get me a flunky job." No one says, "I really want to be a goon, a duct taper, or perhaps a box ticker or a taskmaster." And that is because how we come to our work is something of a process, a journey. Sometimes that journey goes as planned and other times it does not. In either case, that journey begins at home, in our families of origin.

***

When the alarm goes off at 5:30 a.m., Ben springs out of bed rested and ready to face the day. It has not always been this way. In past years, he has had to drag his tired body from the bed. Each morning he and his wife have breakfast together, where they read their daily devotions. Then Ben heads to the woodshop at a monastery, where he works alongside the brothers of a Catholic order.

Ben crafts and sells caskets and urns. Not exactly a job one dreams up, but not a "bullshit" job either.

The first time I met Ben, he told me the story of how he decided to go to college, where he eventually majored in marketing.

---

3 Graeber, *Bullshit Jobs*, 28–52.

Born in the Midwest, he was the oldest of three children. At age seven, his parents divorced, and the courts gave custody of the children to his father, an unusual ruling at the time. They moved from state to state as his father sought out opportunities to provide for the family. After a few years down South, they returned to the Midwest just in time for Ben's senior year of high school.

> *I wanted to go to a state college that could be affordable because my father and I were paying for it. I started out as an accounting major and switched to marketing. I figured marketing was broad enough. I could use it for a lot of different things. My dad was a window salesman. So sales was a natural fit for me.*

The way Ben connects his work to his father's is not uncommon. In fact, I was surprised how often this was the case. Farmers taking over the farm that had been in the family for generations. Medical professionals whose father or mother inspired them to dedicate their lives to helping others. A grandmother who taught her granddaughter apprentice to cut hair.

Long before we learn the vocational script, the one that says God is calling you, it seems that it is our families of origin that teach us about what counts as "good work."

The scripts we learn from our families are inevitably marked by expectations, the high hopes of our parents, and the social imaginations we learn there. They are also marked by the opportunities that our families can or cannot provide for us. So it is not surprising that when we tell stories about how we came to our work, we often describe them as inevitable matters of fate, or self-justifying stories of good intentions.

These stories, ones like "my dad was a salesman," become part of our repertoires, a part of the collection of stories we tell about our lives, long before we learn at church that God, too, might have something to say about our career choices. It's not surprising that many people do not, in fact, view their work as a calling. And for those who do view their work that way, it is often a theological script that has entered the scene alongside other family scripts that run deeper into our past.

It is certainly possible that God is just as much at work in our family scripts as in the vocational script. But there is a noticeable difference between the two. Often our family scripts about the meaning of work function to limit the possibilities of what counts as good work. The vocational script, on the other hand, begins and ends with a wide-open horizon: all work has the potential to be a calling. Our family scripts are written for a life within limits; the vocational script is written within God's limitless horizon.

***

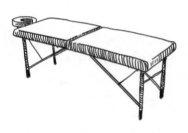

"Women Aren't Doctors"

My parents wanted my brothers and me to have every opportunity possible, and they wanted us to have the freedom to choose our own paths in life. They more than did their part. My parents did not dabble very much in the American Dream narrative. Their imagination for our future had little to do with that national story of exceptionalism. Yet, the message was similar: you can be whatever you want to be.

They could say this to their children for several reasons. My father's well-paying job in healthcare administration provided us with good educational opportunities, first through private schools during our secondary education and later on through college. It was a privileged childhood in that way.

Equally important, however, is that my family could safely assume that the four of us boys would have the privileges white men from well-educated backgrounds could count on. "You can be whatever you want" was a story they could tell without qualifications, not because we boys possess unique *qualifications* but because society was structured that way. When it came to privilege, our American culture dealt my brothers and I a stacked deck, an inherently winning hand. Learning and unlearning the implications of this has been its own kind of work; work that is very much unfinished.

***

When I met Laura and she told me how she came to be a chiropractor in her small Midwestern town, I was struck by the gendered narrative she inherited from her family, part of a whole genre of stories that so many encounter. Stories that turn my family's narrative ("you can be anything you want") into a myth.

> *I had always wanted to be a medical doctor, but my mother said, "Women are not medical doctors. They're nurses." So I went to the [flagship state university] to nursing school. I told her I'd go for a year. And I went for like twelve months and two days [laughter]. It wasn't for me.*
>
> *In the process of working in the hospital, I had seen a lot of things I did not like, how patients were treated, how doctors thought they were better than anyone else. One day I was there for the death of five people. I was the technician on call, and we lost [silence]—so that was really hard for me to get my head around.*

This episode from Laura's story was one of many on the way to her current work as a chiropractor. She grew up in a small Midwestern town, where her father was a self-employed truck driver and her mother managed the bookstore at the local college. After high school, she attended that same local college (tuition free) before heading to nursing school. When she left nursing school after the first year, she began working at the local hospital, eventually landing a job as a dialysis technician.

Laura's father had long seen a chiropractor; hour and hours of long-haul truck driving had taken a toll on his back. Around this time, her mother also started seeing the chiropractor, and soon, her lifelong struggle with headaches got better. When Laura started seeing the same doctor, her headaches got better too. She wasn't really sure what it was a chiropractor did, but she did know that her whole family was experiencing healing. Perhaps a chiropractic practice was the change of pace she needed?

Before she could pursue it fully, she fell in love with a Canadian hockey player. They got married, but things were turbulent and soon the short-lived marriage ended. Or so she thought.

Laura moved to St. Louis for chiropractic college. Her estranged husband showed up for her graduation, which reignited the relationship. Together they moved back to Canada. There, in short order, they had a son and a daughter. It was the first December after her daughter was born that her husband was diagnosed with a rare form of cancer. Just nine months later, he died. Suddenly she was a single parent with little opportunity for employment in a country still quite foreign to her.

Eventually, she was able to return to her hometown in the Midwest to start her chiropractic practice and raise her kids with her parents nearby. In time she also remarried.

When I asked Laura if her Christian faith had impacted her work as a chiropractor, this is what she told me:

I felt like I had the gift of the physicality of the job because it is very physical, manual labor. I did feel like God led me there, and that's what he had intended for me to do. I just had to take this different route before I got there. I think absolutely he was in charge of that.

I felt like during the training that of my schooling and everything that those physical things, not the academics, came easier for me, like learning how to actually do the manipulations. I remember the first day the teacher said, "Well by the end of this class, you'll be able to feel a hair through three-hundred pages on a book." "Oh yeah," I went, "Not possible," but you can. I think that some never did, but I think God had been preparing me with my abilities for that calling. I think absolutely that was what I was supposed to do. It's a good thing he didn't call me to be a preschool teacher.

***

At first glance, it may seem obvious that Laura understands her work as a calling and a way her God-given gifts serve the healing of others. Today, that might be true for Laura, but still, what should we say theologically about the whole trajectory of the story?

Laura's story, like others, includes a series of episodes. It is tempting to conclude Laura's story fits the vocational script. After all, in the end, it seems clear that Laura has found her calling in life. Yet, many of the other episodes are much more difficult to square with the script.

The very first episode, "Women aren't medical doctors; they are nurses," might have been acceptable in Luther's medieval context, but today, if we draw on another of Luther's insights, we can embrace our inner theologians of the cross, call a thing what it is, and call out such gendered narratives for what they really are: *Sin.*

Despite Laura's ultimate vocational clarity, her story begins in the shadows of structural sin. That exchange with her mother was followed by years where Laura endured traumatic experiences for which she was unprepared and that did not fit her gifts. Then just as she began to make her own way, a complicated relationship took over and gender roles again took center stage. During her years living in Canada, Laura struggled with the oppressive and gendered expectations of her late husband, who felt entitled to demand that nearly every waking hour of Laura's day be dedicated to household work and serving his needs. Her life could be mapped by these episodes:

Episode 1: Gendered Expectations
Episode 2: Gendered Expectations Lead to Trauma
Episode 3: Romantic Love Leads to More Gendered Expectations

And then, out of nowhere, cancer and death.

Episode 4: Alone, a Single Mother

It is only at this point that Laura returns to her chiropractic practice and, while it is true that this path would eventually lead her to a place of deep purpose and meaning, I wonder what theologians should make of all these prior episodes. Is this the way our theologies should work? As long as they apply in the finale, then the rest are dismissible?

Furthermore, for every Laura out there, for every story that may take a "different route," there are many others who do not ever find that place of clarity where their working lives are expressions of their giftedness serving the needs of others. If this is the best our theologies can do, where does that leave God? Certainly, God is not only implicated at the end. Certainly, God's presence is not limited to those episodes that positively affirm our vocational script.

It was not clear that Laura was "born to be a chiropractor." And unlike James, Laura did not have encouraging family members pointing out her gifts. Unlike Ben, Laura could not simply join the family business. The terrain on the way to Laura's sense of call was much more difficult, much more painful. How might the church and its theology accompany disciples in all of everyday life, not just the episodes that conform to some predetermined script?

***

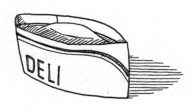

The School of Hard Knocks

Growing up in my family, college was an expectation, and I do not remember considering any other pathway to a career. That alone says something about the complex ways things like family histories and social class shape the work we choose.

A high-achiever friend of mine in high school also grew up with this expectation. During our senior year, as college decisions drew near, she was considering a long list of schools. She was always going to get into all of them, so the question was simply which one she would choose. Her father (an engineer by training) sat her down, and together they came up with a formula for weighing a long list of considerations: location, prestige, cost, facilities, opportunities outside of academics, and so on. They turned the decision into an exact science. I am confident that no one else I know made a more rationally sound college decision than she did.

Me on the other hand? I managed to complete just a single application before the early decision deadlines came and went. When my acceptance letter arrived, I was in the middle of completing all the other applications I had put off. "Wait," I thought to myself, "if I choose this college where I am already accepted, then I will not have to finish these applications."

It was decided.

***

Do we choose our work or does our work choose us?

Most of us live with something like the spirit of individualism, a certain degree of belief that we are autonomous, rational human beings with an agency of our own. We prefer to think that our lot in life is the product of our own making. So we tell stories about ourselves in ways that emphasize the choices we make and minimize those things that are completely out of our control. This is normal. But it is reflective of what one theorist has written about storytelling: "All stories are, in a sense, untrue."[4]

The more I listen to stories others share about their working lives, the more surprised I am that the plot lines of these stories depend on random events, chance encounters, and sheer luck as much as anything else.

It is true, of course, that some people do indeed carefully plan their career choices. Some people clearly do choose their work. However, many others have fallen into their working lives by chance. One way to make sense of these arbitrary developments is to say that they happen as a matter of destiny.

---

4 Michael Jackson, *The Politics of Storytelling: Variations on a Theme by Hannah Arendt* (Copenhagen: Museum Tusculanum Press, 2013), 14.

I tried hard to become a band director, but here I am a theologian. If I am honest with myself, exactly how this came to be the case is only partially based on my own doing.

At the time of the Reformation, when the vocational script came into its own, social mobility was nearly impossible, and the idea of one choosing one's work was terribly uncommon. In such a context, referring to one's working life as a matter of destiny or divinely ordered was a way of making sense of things far beyond one's control. Today, one of the challenges of the vocational script is that it has become a way of justifying our career choices—a way of conflating our agency with God's as if God has a single occupation pre-determined for each and every one of us.

Despite living in a culture that appears to encourage career choice, many today still live stories that seem to defy the notion that we first discern God's will for our working lives and then answer the call.

***

Consider, for example, the story of John, who spent decades learning his trade at the School of Hard Knocks. During high school, it was a school counselor who initially pulled him aside and encouraged him to consider pursuing a trade rather than attending college. Apparently, his educational performances were not very convincing.

My father worked three jobs. I have two brothers and a little sister. There were four of us. My mother stayed at home and raised us. My father was a baker by trade. But to be able to give us the ability to own a home and all that kind of stuff, he worked three jobs (all bakery related). So he wasn't around too much. He consulted for a company that he bought all the baking products from. And so, he probably, I would say, he probably worked sixteen hours a day.

I've been working for a grocery chain since I was 16 years old and started by washing dishes and learning to communicate with people. In other words, sell that product. I work in a meat department. I have a meat-cutting trade.

[Meat cutting] became very easy for me—it was exactly what I was looking for in my life.

But then again, I didn't have a hard time. Our grandparents were farmers, so I didn't have a difficult time cleaning out the barn stalls. The work was easy. Clean up dishes, pick up after some of the full-time meat cutters, actually carry carcasses of beef in the coolers, just—yeah, stuff that people really didn't want to do. Stay on Saturday night, clean the whole case, and sanitize it. A lot of stuff like that. [Pauses] Graduated from high school; had no formal education other than high school. Some people call it the school of hard knocks, by working that way. That was the start of it. Mentors that I had showed me how lucrative the salary was. This corporation is a family-owned business, been around for seventy-eight years. They like to bring people, starting them out from scratch, to upper management, where I am today.

High school years were a lot of trying to find myself: peer pressure, a lot of that. I have a brother who has a PhD, but he's a full-blown schizophrenic, has a lot of problems when he doesn't take his medications. He was a super-achiever, extremely intelligent, almost to the Rain Man *genius type thing. He's a biochemist who now lives in the same community that we do. As I was trying to follow his footsteps, trying to make my own niche, this job became very easy. It was something where I could really put my focus, and that I could really, if I worked hard, make an impression on people, and maybe try to be put into a group of people where they select managers out of.*

***

John may have spent decades trying to find his own way without the kinds of opportunities a college education affords, but today he is a very successful manager. He would often talk about how grateful he was for the mentors who opened doors for him. He would often say that as a manager now, he always tries to spend some time getting to know his employees on a personal basis.

He even did this with me. Our interviews always began and ended with him asking me how my family was doing and how the research was going. John, I learned, was also a very committed volunteer leader in his local congregation. It was easy for me to imagine that God might be at work in John's mentoring—both at work and at the church. But, when I asked John if he ever thought about his work as a calling, he said: "Well now that you mention it. Yeah, maybe."

It was at this moment that I began to have my doubts about vocation's prescriptive potential. Perhaps the vocational script is better suited for life review than career planning.

College Dropout

In the American world of work today, education and work are intrinsically connected. And in many middle- and upper-class families, like the one I grew up in, going to college is an expectation and a *rite of passage*. There is, of course, good reason for this. A recent study from the Brookings Institute[5] reported the following average earnings over a career by educational attainment:

High School Degree or GED	$36,000
Some College, No Degree	$42,000
Associate Degree	$48,000
College Degree (average of all majors)	$68,000

Our market-based economy demands well-educated and highly skilled workers. To keep up with this demand, the world of work is largely shaped by a system of credentialling. Those who are *qualified* get the best jobs. Or, at least, that is the story we often tell about the relationship between qualifications and work, even if we know that is not always the way it really works.

***

Leslie is the vice president of human resources at distribution company. However, her path to the executive suite was anything but typical. In fact, it is probably a path that would be nearly impossible to replicate nowadays.

Growing up, Leslie's father was an architectural draftsman and her mother worked for the state legislature. Her father had earned a professional certification and her mother had gone to a two-year teacher's college—two pathways that were common as they entered their careers. As the oldest, Leslie would have been

---

5 https://www.brookings.edu/blog/up-front/2020/10/08/major-decisions-what-graduates-earn-over-their-lifetimes/.

the first from her middle-class family to graduate from a four-year university.

But as she tells it, Jesus got in the way.

She had grown up in her parents' "liberal intellectual" congregation, but when a few of her friends started going to a non-denominational church, she was intrigued.

> *The church was on fire! It was just so on fire. So I accepted Jesus as my Lord and Savior in that church and surrendered my life, and everything changed for me at that point. I was nineteen and just started seeing everything differently. From the moment that happened, I felt like I have been given a scripture that showed my purpose. I had a hunger and thirst for studying the Bible. And I knew I wanted to teach.*
>
> *But I had a full scholarship to [local private university], and I walked away from that because my focus had changed. I wanted to go to Wheaton, which was kind of the Midwestern school at the time for non-denominational people. And my parents wouldn't allow it. So I did one year at [another private college], and then I dropped out and just got really involved in the church there. Just absorbed everything I could. I floundered because I still lived at home and everything; my parents just couldn't understand what had happened to me. They just couldn't understand. They were in that traditional church, and this was really non-traditional. But then my sister started going there. And just all of that evolved. So I never did graduate from college, but I did marry a Christian guy and started living a Christian life and worked him through school.*

In 1990, the former president of the distribution company recruited her to come work for him.

I told him I would only come to work for him if I could get into human resources because at the time, it was very hard to get into, and I didn't have a degree in it. But I really felt like that's where my strengths were.

He agreed, and so her human resources career began. One year later she was propelled to the very top when the head of human resources transferred to the parent company. Leslie convinced the president to give her a chance and three decades later, she has been a corporate officer under seven different presidents.

Not only is Leslie a human resources executive, but she is also a gifted teacher. Ever since her dramatic conversion, she has taught others about her Christian faith. At her current church, she leads a prayer ministry that teaches others about different ways to pray and deepen their relationship with God. Before that, when her bosses allowed it, she led women's Bible studies over the lunch hour at the office.

A lot of those women came to a much stronger faith. One of them. She and her whole family got saved.

Leslie's personal faith is an integral part of her working life.

I don't hide my faith. They all know where I am.

***

Several things have stuck out since I first heard Leslie's story. First, it's an unlikely story that doesn't fit a normal script. I do not know very many people who have such powerful experiences of Jesus and the church in their young adulthood that they drop everything to be more involved in their faith. Most people, including

Leslie, would probably not suggest dropping out of college when you have a full scholarship and a bright future. That may not be a winning career plan. But it her case, it worked! Not only was Leslie convincing at the beginning of her tenure in HR, but she has also continued to serve in that same role through many leadership transitions. Clearly, she is really good at her job.

Second, the way Leslie explicitly practices her faith *at work* is uncommon. By all accounts, she does this in a discerning way—one that takes seriously her faith commitments and her work responsibilities. That is a tough balancing act. Leslie shared one story about a woman who came to her because she was struggling. She knew Leslie was a person of deep faith and so she asked her how to pray. Leslie also shared with me the isolation she often felt at executive retreats. Many of the other corporate officers avoided her at these social events, assuming she would not approve of everything they said or did.

And I probably wouldn't, she said. Her witness at work has borne fruit, but it has also had its costs.

Leslie's story is one example of how faith and work *can* come together in meaningful ways. Not everyone can explicitly practice their faith at work, and not everyone has the gifts for teaching that Leslie does. Still, under the surface, there is something even more interesting and perhaps even *theological* about Leslie's story.

The world of work today often tells a story about whose work matters the most. That story goes like this: those who are most deserving get rewarded most. That's the *logic of the market.* It's a merit-based system that places a premium on our ability to judge who is the best fit for the job that is available. Even though opportunities to get qualified are not equally distributed to all, the story we often hear at work is that it does not matter who you are, but what you can do. It is not difficult to notice how Leslie's lived experience defies this common narrative. No one could claim, at the beginning, that she was qualified for the position she took on.

When I read the Scriptures, it appears that God does not follow the logic of the market. In fact, God often seems to choose the unqualified like Leslie. Abraham and Sarah were not the right age. Moses did not have the right words. David had a few, well, let's call them character flaws. Naomi did not have the right marital status (neither did the Samaritan woman), and all the disciples come off as more-than-a-little dense.

This pattern in Scripture is part of the very gospel we proclaim: God chooses us *not* because of what we have done or even what we will do, but because of who we are as children of God. The world of work prioritizes what you do rather than who you are. God says the opposite.

This tension between God's logic and the logic of the market causes me to have real questions about many of the stories we tell ourselves. I wonder what it means that, in our working lives, we regularly tell ourselves and each other a story about the meaning and significance of our work that infrequently matches reality. We know from our experience that the winners and losers of the market often have little to do with qualifications. And yet we choose to tell this story anyway. Perhaps we tell this story about the most qualified getting the best opportunities because it taps into our implicit sense of justice, our desire for a world that is fair. Or perhaps we tell this story for less noble purposes. Maybe it is just more convenient for those of us with recognizable "qualifications" to preserve our places of privilege with this self-justifying myth.

Whatever our motivation for telling this story, God does not seem to buy it. God appears steadfast in God's commitment to those we deem unworthy.

This may or may not be great news for me. My profession especially insists that it be governed by a merit-based system. Academics are the ultimate purveyors of qualifications and credentials. We really do believe that we are capable of creating a just system of rewards based on merit, and we have a high degree of confidence in our ability to judge the contributions of others accurately and objectively. My world of work has taken this story about the importance of qualifications and credentials and turned it into employee manuals complete with promotion committees and elaborate ceremonies to accompany it all. We theological educators are no exception. We go along with all of this as if it in no way contradicts the very gospel we have been called to teach.

All of us, even we theologians, have been dangerously miseducated in this way.

"I'm an Accidental Banker"

It was in late September when I got an email from my friend Nadia. We had met through an online discussion forum but became friends while I was doing a summer internship in Colorado. We were both involved in a group that was trying to experiment with new kinds of faith communities.

"A group of us are going to be meeting in San Antonio next week with some bigwig leaders from the national church. You need to be there."

In order to attend, I would have had to skip class. I was in my final year of college, so naturally, I was usually looking for some reason to skip class, and hanging out with Nadia was always a trip.

"I'm in," I said.

Over the course of the next two days, that group gathered in a coffee shop. Mostly, we just told stories from our faith communities. Those two days changed the entire trajectory of my life. Nearly all the most important aspects of my life today can be traced to that singular decision to skip class and hang out with Nadia.

I had spent three years working toward a career in music. Not anymore, though I did not quite know that right away.

During those two days, I met a leader from the national church who recruited me and several other young leaders to start a new church. That invitation eventually led to a part-time role leading the new ministry. As it turns out, ministry is really hard and, if given the chance, many people today have significant questions about God, faith, and the church; questions I was not prepared for, much less ready to address. So I began a seminary program while continuing my work in ministry.

Turns out, I loved seminary.

It also turns out that full-time ministry and full-time graduate studies can be a recipe for disaster. After only a year of trying to make that work out, I left the ministry work for full-time study. I was convinced I would continue my studies for three more years and become a pastor.

But that didn't happen either.

To my complete surprise, by the time I finished seminary, I was applying to doctoral programs in theology. A few years before, I was looking for every opportunity to skip my classes. Now I was signing up for four more years. How did *this* happen?

While some careers are planned, just as many—if not, more—are not. If I am honest, I became a theologian by chance. My entrance into church work was on a whim. My chances of getting into a doctoral program were not very good. Statistically speaking, my chances of finishing and actually getting a job in higher education were even worse.

The fact that many major life events occur by chance or accident has significant implications for how we make such moments meaningful. We employ storytelling as a way of converting the sometimes senseless contingencies of our lives into something that makes sense to us and others. As we craft our life stories, we transform ordinary and random events into purposeful turning points and trajectories. Doing so, however, seems to present a real challenge to the idea that some working lives are inevitable. It also raises the question: *How do we account for these accidents and chance encounters?*

Despite the temptation to narrate our working lives as the outcome of our intentions, some tell quite different stories about how their work began. For example, take a banker I met named Mitch. He was quite upfront about it saying, "I am an accidental banker."

***

Mitch grew up in a fairly large family of six. As he tells it, his mother had him and two of his siblings (a fourth came later) rather early on. "We were raised by children," as Mitch puts it. Despite not having a college education, Mitch's father went on to have a successful career in a major avionics company. Mitch's older brother completed just a single year of college before joining the Air Force, so that left him as the first to complete college.

Early on during those college years, Mitch had a plan. It just was not to be a banker:

> *I was kind of on a premed track. That's what I wanted to do. I chose [the small private liberal arts college] because they had a really strong premed program. And it was that nice two-hour distance from [hometown]. Not too far away. But loved the campus, played basketball there, and I mean, I remember going on campus and almost immediately had a feeling that that was the place to be. And I used that same story when I helped my two daughters make their college selections when they were all wrapped around a pole wondering what their*

friends were doing and was this the right decision—I said,
"You'll know. You'll just know."

At one point, however, Mitch began to doubt he was really cut out for medical school. He worried his GPA would not be high enough (despite the fact that he had a pretty good GPA!), and so he went to visit his academic advisor. Together they realized he was only a few classes away from a major in math. So that's what he did.

But at that moment, there was still no real career plan. Fortunately, employers were beginning to visit campus that spring:

> *I'm an accidental banker because IBM had come to [campus] and said, "We're going to take one person [laughter]." And I went through seven interviews with IBM. And they finally came back to me. Now this would have been 1982 [. . .], So they came back and said, "Hey, congratulations. You're the guy. By the way, we have a hiring freeze." And I'm going, "What?" So upon graduation, I was back [in hometown] and quickly determined after maybe living at home for a week—I was reminded by my dad, "Probably you should look for a job." Yeah, I suppose I should. And went to work for a finance company. Progressed pretty quickly with them. And soon, about three years after that, shortly before we got married, I made the switch and did my first bank job. And after that it's been fun ever since, but very accidental. Did not have any intentions of getting into banking. But I've enjoyed it.*

Mitch tells this story with a certain degree of admirable humility, but the fact is that today, Mitch is a regional president of one of the top five largest banks in the United States. Within his industry, he is at the very top of his game, *and he got there by accident.*

It is an uncomfortable truth, but despite the metanarratives we tell about our working lives (e.g., the American Dream) and despite our best intentions, the origins and trajectories of many working lives are a complete fluke. They might have happened. They might not have.

Mitch could have been a doctor.

Mitch could have been a programmer or an executive at IBM.

Mitch could have ended up in finance his entire career.

But Mitch is an *accidental* banker.

That is how it worked out, even if it very well could have gone a different way.

***

In its classic form, our vocational script seems to suggest a certain kind of inevitability for our working lives. After all, if God does indeed call us to *particular* callings, then God must have a certain kind of intention for our work, whether we realize it or not. And unless God comes up with these intentions on a whim, then God must have a divine vocational plan for each and every one of us. Or I suppose it is possible that God has a divine vocation plan for *some*, but the rest of us are on our own.

I want to propose another possibility altogether.

What if the voice of God is not singular and, therefore, God's call on our lives is not singular either? Luther himself was quite clear that we have multiple vocations; each relationship, role, or identity we take on comes with its own vocational potential. If that multiplicity is implied across Luther's vocational thinking, then we can also extend that multiplicity into our working lives. Perhaps God is less interested in being some kind of divine career planner. Perhaps instead God can see all the contingencies of our everyday lives—the divergent paths, the could-have-beens, and the might-have-beens—and remain committed to work in, with, and through our working lives, no matter how it all turns out.

The version of God I have in mind here is a dynamic and responsive one. This God is not limited by a singular path our lives *ought* to take. Rather, God embraces a certain degree of randomness and God tolerates much more ambiguity than we do. This does not suggest that God does not delight with those who pursue their working lives with careful planning or intentions. And this does not suggest that God is uninvolved among those who have longstanding clarity of purpose in their work. But it is to suggest that this is not the *only* way God is active in the unfolding of our working lives. God works in, with, and through our working lives, but often God does so in ways that are much more limited and much more complex than the classic vocational script can account for.

***

This most certainly *is* good news for me (and many others I know) because being a professional theologian means existing in a world of work that is unpredictable. I cannot be sure I will always have the opportunity to teach, do research, and work with my colleagues to build faith-based institutions of higher education. And so if this ends, I can be confident that I will find a way to respond to that. And so will God.

"A Natural Fit"

In my early twenties, while serving a mission congregation, the bishop assigned me a mentor, a veteran pastor who served a large church in Austin, Texas. Every few weeks we would meet to talk about the challenges of full-time ministry. One week I brought up a frustrating situation—the kind that did not have any easy answers.

I really just wanted to vent about it. But rather than sympathizing with me, the pastor said:

"Well, what are you going to do if this doesn't work out? What's your plan B?"

"If what doesn't work out?" I asked.

"All of it. What would you do tomorrow if you couldn't lead this ministry anymore or ever for that matter?"

At the time, I thought the question was annoying. I was just looking for someone to agree with me. In the days that followed, this pastor's probing question just would not leave me alone. In an effort to exorcise the question from my daily thoughts, I sat down at the computer and wrote out a plan B—a sort of doomsday scenario for what I would do if I could no longer be in ministry.

Strangely, it was liberating. Having an idea of possibilities beyond those things that most immediately demanded my attention gave me a sense of freedom: freedom to fail, freedom to not know what I was doing, freedom to do something really hard (e.g. start a church), and perhaps most importantly, freedom to let it all go and do something else.

***

When I first met Caroline, she told me about the first half of her working life—twenty years spent as a fitness instructor and physical education teacher. She showed up to the interview having come straight from a workout. Having an active lifestyle was very important to her; it's who she is.

Growing up, her physical education teacher at school was a mother figure and role model for Caroline. When her parents divorced, it set off a season of insecurity. She continued to live with her father, who remarried and divorced again three times. In college, Caroline studied education and afterwards took a year-long substitute position as a physical education teacher. Because it was quite difficult to get a long-term position in the local school district, Caroline taught classes at a fitness center while she and her husband started their family. Once the kids were a little older, she was able to secure a position in the school district.

As she continued in her career, however, Caroline wondered if she should be a physical education teacher her entire career. And that's when Caroline experienced something of a crucible moment:

> *My dad died when I was in my early forties. I think up to that time, I felt that there was just a little bit more infinite ending to life. He died at sixty-nine, so I just kind of went, "You know what? There's a lot of things that I said I was going to do. And I haven't done them."*
>
> *So I got my master's in education in administration, thinking that I wanted to go that route because I knew that teaching physical education for the long term, I just didn't think that was a good idea for the students' best interests and mine. Because I knew a lot of physical education teachers, [I knew] that if you can't demonstrate, you can't participate, you can't do some of those things; then you need to let somebody else to come along. In that process, I soon learned that [administration] was going to be a very lonely profession because you don't have a lot of camaraderie or relationships again. I kind of already experienced that with physical education. So anyway, I got my masters. I continued to teach.*
>
> *And then, on my list was this potential for real estate. My brother-in-law's a home builder. My dad tried several times to get his real estate license. But at the time, you couldn't use a calculator. You had to do everything by hand,*

math-wise. And so, he just never could get the math. I just
had a fascination with houses. We personally had purchased,
fixed up, and sold three homes, I think, at that time. I didn't
use a real estate agent. So anyway, I just kind of had a little
bit of fascination with it. I wasn't extremely happy with
the teaching piece because of my teaching partner and my
principal at the time. I thought, "I'm going to get my real
estate license and give it a whirl."

Over time, Caroline eventually transitioned to a full-time real
estate agency as a second career. Hearing Caroline tell her story,
it seemed to me that there was a profound connection between
her early life—marked by an unstable home life—and the second
act of her work story. It was almost as if she was redeeming that
difficult chapter of life through her work as a real estate agent.
When I asked her about this possible connection, she said:

For me, [real estate] was a natural fit because my home is
extremely important to me. I didn't have a stable home when
I was younger, so I probably have an unhealthy relation-
ship with my house [laughter] because I have a really hard
time moving, even though we have moved a few times. I
don't want to be without a happy, comfortable home. And
I think that other people should have a happy, comfortable
home as well.

Caroline's second act as a real estate agent allowed her to
pursue a deeply held passion, but it wasn't one that was there all
along. It had its roots in her early childhood, but the specifics only
developed over time. It is possible to imagine that Caroline chose
to pursue her career in real estate because she felt called to it. But
that's not the story she tells. If you ask Caroline, she may tell you
that she still doesn't know what she's supposed to be when she
grows up. More than anything else, she is clear about her calling

to be a mother. Both her professional careers had connections to that central sense of calling. Her teaching career was influenced by a mother figure and her real estate career was related to her passion for creating homes that were safe and stable places, which is exactly what good parents want for their children. Still, Caroline wouldn't describe those careers as a calling. It just didn't quite fit.

***

Theologians today often resist the urge to conflate vocation with occupation. But despite their best efforts, when we talk about "work," we most often mean *paid* work; we mean jobs and careers. This makes sense, of course, and yet there is a shadow side to our tendency to forget about the range of work that goes unpaid. Here I think especially about domestic work, things like keeping a household running and raising children. There's no doubt that these things are work. In fact, nearly all the tasks involved are ones that others are paid to do in other situations.

How many careers are underwritten by the unpaid work of supportive spouses? Too many to count, for sure! Part of the shadow side is that this kind of work is left unacknowledged, but perhaps even more poignant is when this work is also under-valued and undercelebrated. Even more problematic, however, is that, traditionally, this is exactly the kind of work that often gets labeled "women's work." Why is it that women's work is the work that is unpaid, unacknowledged, undervalued, and undercelebrated?

Why isn't Caroline's calling to be a mother valued in the same way that any paid work would be? It's hard to imagine that this is the way God would organize our work. Certainly, God seeks to accomplish God's work through us, whether we are paid for those hours or not. Certainly, God does not think about some work as "women's work" and some as "men's work." Those are stories we tell about the division of labor, but given the persistent inequality in that arrangement, it is safe to assume that God does not endorse such an engendered version of work's purpose and meaning.

Luther's writings on vocation have significant liabilities, but Luther is clear that vocation transcends this distinction between paid and unpaid work. Actually, for Luther, the kind of work that happens at home is the very cornerstone of a society. In addition to considering marriage itself a vocation, Luther saw the work of raising a family as one of the most important callings. It is at home that we first learn to love, to serve, and to forgive others. The home, then, is a sending community. That is, from our homes where we first learn how to practice Christian ways of love, we are sent into the world. As one Lutheran theologian put it, "For its closely-knit members, [the home] is a society in embryo: a combination church, state, court, hospital, schoolroom, and playground all in one."[6]

Given all the value narratives and metanarratives that we pick up as Americans today, it is still difficult for many of us to value unpaid work in this way. If you need more evidence of this, just ask the women in your lives. They will tell you.

***

I didn't end up needing that plan B document I wrote all those years ago. I'm glad I didn't because while I would like to believe that I would have been willing to let go of everything and embrace a second act, I don't know if I could have done it. That hasn't stopped me (yet!) from continuing my practice of writing out those plans. My current work as an academic theologian is precarious at best. So I have a plan B and even a plan C. God only knows if I will ever need them, and despite my own trepidation

---

6 William H. Lazareth, *Luther on the Christian Home: An Application of the Social Ethics of the Reformation* (Philadelphia: Muhlenberg Press, 1960), 144.

about it, I hope that if there comes a time when I need to walk away, I will have Caroline's confidence to start all over again.

"It's What I Knew"

My first job was bussing tables at an Italian restaurant. I was sixteen. My father thought we boys needed summer jobs, and as school wrapped up, his pressure campaign began. One day, on the way home from a church meeting, he stopped by that restaurant to speak with the manager. He brought me an employment application and informed me that I had an interview the next day.

If I remember correctly, the interview with the manager—a tall, slender man named Sly—was a bit of a formality. I don't think they hired many people pawned off on them by their parents. Nonetheless, I was hired on the spot.

I don't mean to brag, but I was a really good busboy. I had all the right attributes: I was fast, efficient, and stayed out of other people's way. We had a competition to see who could carry the most glasses at once from the dining room to the dish pit. I won by balancing two stacks of eight glasses in each hand for a total of thirty-two glasses.

I still give my father a hard time about that, but the truth is I really enjoyed working there. I loved the buzz of a Saturday service—the servers bouncing between their tables and the computer stations where they'd place orders into the system. I loved helping the servers out by refilling drinks and taking away finished plates. I got quite a few extra tips that way. I loved the sound of the kitchen—cooks yelling out orders and instructions and the clanking of pots and pans on those industrial stovetops.

I also loved the freedom that came with earning my own money. I no longer had to ask my parents for the things I wanted. I regularly bought things my parents wouldn't have gotten me just because I could.

There were some really bad services, like the time a line cook threw tomatoes into a hot pan of oil, producing a massive fire ball. It was a neat trick, but it set off the fire suppression system, and for some reason, no one could figure out how to turn it off. You wouldn't believe how much water those things put out.

But there were really good services too, when the camaraderie was on point and a lot of guests left happy. I could probably write an entire book of stories just from those two years working at the restaurant. It is not surprising that even though I was very good at bussing tables, it never occurred to me that God might be calling me to be a busboy.

***

Mary told me she has a gift for cutting hair. Her grandmother was a hairdresser, and she taught Mary the tools of the trade. Growing up, Mary had a dream of being an architect. Twice she tried college, but both times it didn't work out, so she enrolled in cosmetology school.

> It was a decision based on—I think I was not being patient. I worried about money. It was one of those things that I could finish faster, took less time than a four-year degree took. In the late '70s and early '80s, it was hard to find a job. Minimum wage was three dollars an hour. But I always regretted not sticking with [college].

By the end of cosmetology school, she married and together with her husband relocated to the Pacific Northwest for his military career. For a time, she stepped away from her work as a hairdresser, but four years after the birth of her first daughter, Mary again turned to her natural talent for cutting hair. Her marriage was headed downhill, and she wondered if she could support herself and her daughter on her own.

I needed to get back out there, even though it's not what I wanted to do. It's what I knew how to do. It helped my self-confidence. It then made me feel like I didn't have to stay in that marriage. I could choose to leave because I could financially support myself. And then, that's when we had the second daughter.

She took off a year to be with her newborn daughter and then went back to work. Around this time, her life took a series of twists and turns. At work, she began to manage the salon she was working at, and eventually she bought her own salon. On the home front, she finalized a divorce and remarried later on. During that second marriage, the work was not fulfilling, but by then, as she describes it, "I didn't know what else I would do." Unfortunately, not long after, injuries from a car accident made full-time hair cutting impossible for her. When I first met Mary, she was only able to work a couple of days a week.

***

There is a long history in Christian theology of connecting vocation to giftedness. In the previous chapter, we learned that Calvin placed a premium on the gifts and abilities of each disciple in his theology of vocation. He was, however, not the first theologian to make this connection. Over a thousand years before, John

Chrysostom, then Archbishop of Constantinople, made a very similar point in a series of sermons reflecting on the role of commerce in Christian life. There he states that God is the very source of our ambitions and abilities. In the eyes of God, says Chrysostom, all labor and talents are equal.

This might have made sense in the fourth century, and perhaps even in sixteenth century, but our market-based economies today value some skills more than others. Certain skills lead to wealth, while others lead to poverty. I am sure there are highly paid workers in the field of cosmetology, but the Bureau of Labor Statistics reported in 2020 that the average pay for barbers, hairdressers, and cosmetologists was about thirteen dollars per hour. That is barely a livable wage for a single person living in Mary's home state. It is not a livable wage to support a family of any size. The outlook for bussers is even worse.

It is one thing to give God credit for our talents and abilities, but it is easy to find oneself in a theological ditch if we take this much further in today's world of work. Doing so can make it seem as if God is some kind of divine card dealer; some get dealt a good hand with in-demand skills, while others are dealt a losing hand. But this cannot be how God works. Certainly, God does not pre-ordain some for economic success and leave others struggling for their very existence.

What if instead, we tried to find God at work in the daily grind of our working lives? What if we just gave up on the idea that it is God behind our successes and failures? What if all of that has more to do with our own human, and therefore, imperfect ways of organizing our economies than it does God's grand design?

I found myself asking these questions as I listened to Mary's story. She has gone through some tough things in her life, and she did so often with few resources and fewer opportunities.

The origin story of her work is much more modest than others. Even if it doesn't make sense to call Mary's work as a hairdresser a "calling," I do think it is possible to see God at work there. It doesn't seem like a stretch to imagine that God was at work as she rediscovered a sense of self-confidence and found the courage to leave a destructive marriage. And if we resist the urge to conflate giftedness with vocation, we can simply say that Mary is good at cutting hair without assuming that just because she is good at it, God is calling her to depend on that gift for her personal well-being. God wants Mary to flourish—full stop.

***

My brief stint in the restaurant industry as a teenager was ultimately more of a gift to me than I was to that restaurant. After a few months, I got the opportunity to work in a different role as an expediter, or "expo" in industry lingo. In a restaurant the front-of-the-house is staffed by hosts, servers, bussers, and the like, while the back-of-the-house is staffed by dishwashers, prep cooks, line cooks, and so on. The expo works between these two groups of staff, coordinating orders between different cooking stations and placing the finishing touches on dishes before they go out to guests.

At that particular Italian restaurant, the front-of-the-house was staffed largely by college students, young adults, and a few college graduates between jobs. For the most part, they came from families and backgrounds like mine. The back-of-the-house staff was a completely different group. Many of the cooks had learned their trades through on-the-job training. Many of them showed up to evening services having already worked one or two shifts elsewhere. Some didn't speak much English; none were actually Italian. Some were in their early twenties, while others were into their sixties.

Coordinating between these two worlds wasn't always easy, but it taught me to value the work of restaurant workers far more than any of their wages. They were all talented. They were all underappreciated. And they were all underpaid.

Side Job

Doctoral-level study in theology is a full-time job, but a few years into my studies, I picked up a side job as an adjunct instructor at a seminary. It was a great opportunity to practice my craft, and I was especially excited because I would be teaching in a program designed for non-professionals. The course went great, and when it was over, I went back to my full-time gig as a student. About a year later, one of my former students wrote to me asking for a letter of recommendation. Our course together had been an important step for her on a longer road of discernment, and she was now ready to pursue full-time ministry. In her email to me, she was tentative in her request: "I know you're probably really busy, so I understand if you don't have the time."

Don't have the time? What are you talking about! These are the very moments we teachers live for—how would I *not* have time to write in support of a student who wanted to take the next step in their education? Besides, she was a great student and writing the letter would be easy.

As I wrote her letter, I was surprised how many emotions came to the surface. It was humbling to be even a small part of that student's journey to ministry. Since then, I've written several letters of recommendation, and each time I'm surprised how rewarding it is to tell others why my students should get whatever opportunity they are pursuing. It's one of my favorite parts of the job, and it is easy to see how God is at work in the relationships involved.

[Fast forward several years]

A few weeks ago, I had a very different experience on the job. I had one of those days that just leaves you asking, Why?

Why are we doing this? Certainly, there is a better way.

Why am I doing this? This isn't what I signed up for.

My questions stemmed from an especially frustrating meeting and several that followed over the next months. If I'm honest, writing letters in support of my students is easy to see as some kind of collaboration with God's work in the world. But you will never convince me that year of pointless monthly meetings had anything to do with the Creator and Sustainer of the universe. It was just bureaucratic nonsense. Being a theological educator today is a mixed bag. Some days you get to change a student's life. Other days you're just a cog in the bureaucratic machine of higher education. That's the job.

***

Karl is first and foremost a farmer. It's hard to tell if he chose farming or if farming chose him. He grew up farming and he grew up Catholic. At one point he was on track to becoming a deacon in the Catholic Church, but his candidacy was tanked when the diocese learned that he had written a book with his sister, an out lesbian. That's about the time he started attending a Lutheran church nearby. I met Karl after his pastor recommended him for participation in my research project.

In addition to my interviews with these workers, I also gave each of them a voice recorder and invited them to share with me reflections from their daily work. Karl embraced the invitation and recorded over twenty daily reflections. In his first recording, he described a typical day on the farm:

> *All right, Tim, we'll give this a shot. In the springtime when I'm tilling the fields, I'll refer it to as, "I'm going to work to till God's garden." It might be a rather large garden, but I feel it to be God's garden. To tend it for all year and to harvest its extreme bounty; and to look at it as we plant 35,000 seeds, and this year we may be looking at in excess of twenty-three million seeds per acre—that's an extreme bounty and I'm very blessed.*
>
> *I was at a four-hour meeting yesterday, where we discussed our year and history as far as challenges for growing a crop and problems that there were and what methods farmers had used to increase that and what they can do differently. Even the speakers referred to our local area, right here, as the garden spot. That's in reference to how everything has lined up as far as weather, timing, capability of getting crop in and out; we are very fortunate in this area. I guess that's why I refer to it as God's garden, and I'm just fortunate to be able to do that, not only to support our own family, but as it travels down the country or down the road, that it supports others as well.*
>
> *And today I'm going to be harvesting some hay that we didn't get done because of weather. Have a short window in the weather, it looks like, from today and tomorrow maybe to get that done before it rains again. And that's always a challenge in farming, that you operate within the weather window to do what you need to*

do, and you hope that works out. All right. Talk to you another time.

Then a few days later, he surprised me with this recording:

This is August 23rd, a Thursday. It is the first day of school for [the local school district], and I went back to another job that I've done for 24 years, and that's a bus driver. I've enjoyed it. I have kids that have been behaving, and I seem to have a way of drawing that out of them. I've been blessed, I think, with the ability to have that kind of patience. I've enjoyed it. Not to say there haven't been some issues, but I think I've been given the ability to reach kids, try to teach them things or lessons that will continue to serve them in life, and steer them in the right way. I feel fortunate that I have been able to do that. I actually started the job when the farm and the economy were struggling, but I've done it more since because I enjoyed it. I think I have a way with kids that I can find them, or they can find me, someone that they can confide in and trust, and the patience that goes along with that.

During our first interview together, he hadn't mentioned his side job.

***

Why do we work? That is one of those existential questions I asked myself as I listened to these workers. For Karl, the answer to that is pretty clear: his work is not just what he does for a living; it is part of how he understands the very demands of his Christian faith to help others.

Of all those I interviewed, Karl was among those who connected their daily work to their faith most clearly. He understands his farming as the opportunity to work God's garden. At this point, he continues to drive the bus to be a positive role model for the kids he takes to and from school. I sincerely wish it were possible for everyone to get up each morning and go to work with this kind of integrated approach to faith and work.

What I learned is that we actually can't all be like Karl. *And that's okay.*

It is tempting to think that the best relationship between one's work and one's faith is an integrated one like Karl's. You can tell that Karl finds significant meaning in his work. You can tell that his faith means a lot to him and that it motivates his work. It causes him to reflect on those who will receive the bounty of his fields and it shapes how he relates to the students on his bus.

There is a subtle danger in thinking that the way Karl understands his work is the way everyone should see their work. That danger is twofold. First, it simply is not the case that God's work depends in any way on our understanding of it. God can, and does, work through us and our work, whether or not we are aware of it. Understanding our work as a calling is not a pre-requisite for God's involvement. If the only stories we tell are ones like Karl's, it can too easily seem as if our understanding is a condition for God's involvement in our working lives.

Second, notice the way Karl talks about the relationship between God's work and his. There's a certain kind of romanticism in play. The fields of his farm are transformed into God's garden. Each bus ride is a masterclass in life skills. This is not a criticism of Karl; it's just the way he experienced these two daily reflections he shared with me. But we all tend to invoke God in the midst of things we find beautiful and virtuous. When work is good, God is clearly involved. When work is bad, God is suddenly absent.

There is nothing wrong, of course, with the way Karl tells his story. This is the way he experiences his work as a farmer and a bus driver. It just can't be the only kind of story we hear—at least if we want to understand the relationship between God's work and ours.

4

Toil

There is a temptation in our culture to talk about work in overly romantic terms, but work will always take its toll on us. We seem to have this fundamental belief that hard work is good work. And while it is true that some very good things are not easily attained, work exacts personal costs. Studs Terkel, the broadcaster and Pulitzer Prize-winning author, wrote over five hundred pages about his interviews with American workers. For his opening line of *Working*, Terkel wrote, "This book, being about work, is, by its very nature, about violence—to the spirit as well as to the body."[1]

That was an extraordinary way to begin the book in 1972 and it is still extraordinary because talking about the violence and cost of our work is taboo. The stories in this section break this strange silence. They include stories about work that is misunderstood and deeply disappointing. They are stories about loneliness, inappropriate and unethical behavior, and even abuse. These things, too, are a part of many working lives.

Such evidence points to our need for new ways of thinking about our working lives that are not unapologetically positive; ways of thinking beyond the vocational script. This script describes stories about work at its best—what follows is anything but that. The vocational script unintentionally diverts our attention to the parts of our work that we tend to find satisfying: helping others, making a difference, or pursuing our passions.

It is problematic to limit our attention to experiences like these because they are only part of the human experience. If it

---

1 Studs Terkel, *Working: People Talk about What They Do All Day and How They Feel about What They Do* (New York: The New Press, 1974), xi.

is not yet clear what's especially theological about this, let me be as clear as possible. The relationship between God's work and ours is not confined to our good days (or months, or years!) at work. Actually, God is especially concerned with a whole range of experiences we often try to avoid. It's in these very experiences where God promises to meet us.

Theologians sometimes refer to this side of God as the *crucified* God. The crucified God is the one who shows up not just in those things we find especially satisfying and life-giving but in the "violence to the spirit and body" as Terkel would say; to those things that bring death. Here we don't just mean the literal end of life, but also all those experiences that rob us of life's abundance. Work is a daily grind, a struggle to get through whatever is immediately in front of us. We need to find ways to talk about God's presence within that daily grind.

The stories that follow are not always easy to read. But if you can, try to stay with them. Even if they tell of work's darker side, they too are not the only stories worth telling. Here we find stories that speak about work's ultimate meaning, but in a wholly Christian way. First, we have to confront the violence and death.

Cashiers in Lab Coats

In today's complex world of work, some professions suffer from being misunderstood by others. Theologians are just one of those professions. Recently on a flight to a conference, I was seated next to a man who was probably in his mid-sixties. We exchanged pleasantries, and then it happened. We theologians know this is an occupational hazard, but it always catches me off guard, nonetheless.

What do you do for work?

At that very moment, I went through this internal dialog with myself. My first instinct is always to lie. *Just make something up, Tim! Tell him you sell insurance. He'll never know.*

One colleague of mine, a Bible scholar, tells people he studies ancient texts because in his experience this will always end the conversation. Another colleague of mine—she teaches Christian Education—will sometimes just say she teaches education so as to avoid the dilemma altogether. It's not untrue. Still another colleague of mine just turns up his grump vibe as high as he can without being unkind. He's never been asked.

My brother, who also happens to be a professor, teaches business. But when he tells people this, it doesn't lead to awkward conversations. If you're a theologian, you know what comes next if you tell a complete stranger what you do for a living. Things often get weird quickly. If you want to know how, just try telling someone you're a theologian sometime.

***

Despite our assumptions about this or that profession, all our work can be somewhat opaque to those who are not in that profession. This may seem obvious, but it is important to point out that for the vast majority of human history, work was not this way. For most of human history, even as work was transformed by the division of labor, the contribution and significance of specialized jobs were clear.

I was unaware what kind of problem this might be until I met Jennifer, a pharmacist. To be fair, I haven't had a lot of experience with pharmacists. Still, it didn't really occur to me that pharmacists play an important safeguarding role within healthcare today. It turns out, I just thought of them as cashiers in lab coats.

I realized that I thought of pharmacists this way when Jennifer told me this story during one of our interviews together.

> *Just this last week, I had a prescription that was "level one," which means you do not dispense these drugs together. The doctor had sent a script for something that the patient shouldn't have. I mean it could have killed them. So I said, "Have a seat, we've got to call them and figure out what they're going to switch it to because we can't give you this."*
>
> *Sometimes the patient's fine with that, but some people get into the mode where 'It should take five minutes and I'm out of here.' And it's like, "No. It's a little more complicated, and we're trying to do the right thing for you."*

In the audio diaries she shared with me, Jennifer told several more stories, including this one, about the role she plays providing direct care to patients:

> *I had a patient who came in for a prednisone prescription, which is a steroid for inflammation. I asked what she was treating, and she showed me her arm. The whole arm was circular red, like shockingly red, huge, swollen, inflamed. I asked what happened, and she said it was an insect bite. And I said, "They didn't give you an antibiotic?" She said, "No. They didn't think they needed to." I literally helped her draw a line on the outside edge of where the redness ended, and I just basically warned her that, "If this doesn't get any better, or if it gets worse, you need to go to the doctor and get a second opinion," because I thought she needed an antibiotic.*

As if saving lives and offering her professional medical advice weren't enough, she also told stories of the role pharmacists play in safeguarding society by ensuring the wrong substances don't end up in the wrong hands:

We had given out a prescription, and the patient was supposed to have the written one with them, and they didn't, or we forgot to ask for it. It's a controlled medication, and so the doctor had called it in, but the patient was supposed to drop off the written one, and we didn't receive it. So technically, the patient could have taken that piece of paper and gone to a different pharmacy and tried to fill it again. It was my job to try to get a hold of the patient and see if they had it. Well, the patient had had surgery. He wasn't moving around very well, and he said he didn't have it. I had to call the doctor's office and say, "Somehow, it got misplaced. We didn't know where the prescription was. Can you write us another prescription?" About an hour later, the patient calls back and says his wife had the written prescription. So we had to call our driver to pick up that piece of paper and bring it back to the pharmacy. Everything was good. You like to believe that people will be honest, but you never know. Because sometimes there's drug-seeking behavior, and people would try to take advantage of that.

After learning about Jennifer's work, I came to understand the critical role pharmacists play on the healthcare teams that provide holistic care to their patients.

***

One of the ways our work becomes meaningful is by giving us new identities. When we become theologians or pharmacists, we take on new self-understandings. In some sense, we are what we do. One of the insidious realities of today's world of work is that so much of who we are as workers remains misunderstood. When pharmacists are thought of as cashiers in lab coats, it's difficult to see them as they really are: as healthcare professionals. Even if Jennifer feels like being a pharmacist is a perfect fit for her, there are days when being misunderstood weighs on her.

If there is some relationship between our work and God's, does it matter that our work is, at times, fundamentally misunderstood?

On the one hand, it doesn't seem as if understanding God's actions is really a prerequisite for its effectiveness. God seems to accomplish all kinds of things despite our level of understanding. So maybe it doesn't matter. Maybe God works behind the scenes whether we recognize the work for what it really is or not. Whether we understand what is going on or not, God may very well be at work as Jennifer safeguards her patients at risk of taking conflicting medications, or as she tracks down a missing prescription.

On the other hand, it does seem like a missed opportunity. I wonder if it would be easier for us to notice God at work in the world if we really understood what each of us were really up to at work. What might happen if we told more stories about our work—the kind of stories that help others see and understand the significance of our work?

***

Because I'm a theologian, it also doesn't feel right to lie straight-up, so in that moment on the airplane, I fumble through some ways to answer without giving away my secret. *I'm a professor. Or, I'm a teacher.* These seem like they would work because they're true enough, but they invite too many follow-up questions. In that moment, I just give up.

I'm a professor—I teach theology and ministry at a seminary.

Oh, he says, turning his attention back to the book he was reading a few minutes before. Believe it or not, this was the best possible outcome.

Unspoken Potential

I showed up a little early for my appointment with the dean and knocked gently on the door. After what seemed like forever, I heard a voice from the corner office:

"Coming."

Moments later the door slowly opened, and he invited me to take a seat on one of the mismatched lounge chairs surrounded by floor-to-wall bookshelves in his cramped faculty office. I bet there were a thousand books in that office.

We began with small talk, and he asked me how my dissertation was going. It was behind schedule and slow. In hindsight, it may have been a mistake to take on full-time academic work just as my research was beginning. Now I had two jobs. But I was close to having a complete draft and there was no turning back. To be honest, I was tired of people asking.

My hands were sweating as I clutched my black leather-bound journal where I kept pages and pages of meeting notes and to-do lists. I brought it along but knew I would not need it. The dean thought this would be just another one of our weekly check-ins, but I had accepted a new position, and I needed to tell him.

Days before as I thought about how I would break the news and how he might react, I remembered a story from Mitch, the accidental banker. Now a top executive at a national bank, Mitch told me a story that he shares with all his managers, a sort of real-life parable about their responsibility as supervisors. He tells them, "Never do this to an employee."

Early in his career, Mitch had accepted an offer to join a banking group in another Midwestern state. He went to the bank president, told him, and said, "I've made this decision and I'll be leaving. How about three weeks?"

To his surprise, the bank president got visibly angry and barked, "You'll never know what your future here was!"

Mitch quipped back, "Well, don't you think that was the problem? You never told me."

At the time, Mitch was just being a smartass (by his own admission!). But as he took on supervisory responsibilities himself, he remembered that moment and imagined how it could be different for those who reported to him. This workplace parable is about a supervisor's responsibility to identify talent and foster that through encouraging conversations that engage an employee's interests and goals. Mitch uses this story to impress on his managers what is at stake: it is their job to develop others. If they don't have these conversations, it's likely their talented younger employees will end up elsewhere.

Time and again in my interviews, workers told me stories about how their colleagues played a part in their personal growth and career advancement. Of course, some also reported that some supervisors got in the way of their growth and development. Many of those I interviewed recognized that the possibility of self-development was a significant part of what they found meaningful about their work.

***

Dan McAdams, a clinical psychologist, describes our development as an unfolding story that we both craft and live. Writing about defining moments, such as the one Mitch experienced with his boss early in his career, McAdams calls these "nuclear episodes."[2] They are moments that initially can seem rather mundane and ordinary, but over time they take on extraordinary significance. Mitch's experience with a bad boss has now become management folklore at a Fortune 500 company.

It seems like a major risk for God to make us dependent on others making an investment in us and reflecting back what they see in us so that we can see that ourselves and become more fully what God intended. Wouldn't it have been easier for us to be fully formed on our own and ready to go on day one?

As I set out to listen to stories from the world of work, I was expecting to hear about great accomplishments and successes. Or, I thought, perhaps workers would tell me that their work was a means to an ends, such as caring for their family or volunteering in their community. I did hear stories like those. For example, I met an administrator whose lab had helped map the human genome, and a farmer told me about mobilizing his community to help immigrant mothers after federal agents conducted a raid at the meatpacking plant in town.

I was less prepared for the stories of self-development, those minor episodes and exchanges that either make work insufferable or a blessing. Much of the meaning of work today comes to us as we encounter others—both those who open doors and those who get in the way. Mitch's boss offered him nothing but silence. Apparently, Mitch was supposed to have read his mind and implemented his unspoken masterplan. Yet, it was precisely this bad experience that provided the source material for decades of Mitch's intentional investment

---

2 Dan P. McAdams, *The Stories We Live By: Personal Myths and the Making of the Self* (New York: The Guilford Press, 1993), 295.

in others. I doubt Mitch would accept that this workplace parable is a theological one. He clearly sees it as simply "good business." And that may be true. It also seems possible that God is at work as Mitch helps chart paths for others' self-development, though it may seem strange or overstated to suggest that God is orchestrating every interaction or conversation in our working lives. Given the variety of tasks and relationships involved in Mitch's job as a bank executive, it may be excessive to claim that God is at work in everything Mitch does at work, but it may be more tenable to imagine that every now and then, God is caring for the wellbeing of others through Mitch's investment in them.

***

The entire conversation lasted about thirty minutes.

As I had suspected, the dean was caught off guard that I would be leaving, and my departure would leave a difficult hole to fill on short notice. The weeks that followed were filled with mixed emotions. I took some time to thank many colleagues who had taken interest in my work and who had invested in my growth as a scholar and a teacher. But I was also leaving a place where I had no future. Only three years before, I had begun my work there during a season of major life changes. In the two months before I started that position, I had moved, gotten married, went on a honeymoon, and moved again—this time across the country. It was an exciting time as I began a career that I had spent years preparing for.

Within months, however, my excitement had given way to a deep disappointment. I had been wrong about the opportunity. Theologians and pastors often think about their work as a vocation, a "calling." To be honest, I am not quite sure how to square the idea that God called me to that place—something I was clear about at the time—with the deep disappointment

I experienced there. Did God think I needed to be disappointed? Maybe the vocational script doesn't fit even us theologians at times. Maybe we also have to improvise and go off script.

Of course, the dean and I didn't talk about that. He graciously thanked me for my contributions to the school and I thanked him for his support. I then took the elevator right outside his door up to the third floor and began to pack up my office.

Liars Wanted

Since I was sixteen, I have worked at a restaurant, a coffeeshop, a chiropractor's office, at four different churches, and four different seminaries. In every instance, I have wanted those jobs. When I met Ben a few years ago, I realized just how privileged my working life has been. Here's ten ways my experience at work might be different from yours:

1. I have never been fired (I did come close twice—one I deserved, the other not so much).
2. With one exception, I have gotten every job I applied for.
3. Each of the full-time positions I've held came with a salary, health care, and retirement benefits.
4. In all twenty years of my working life, I have been able to take vacations or time away from work. And I have.
5. I have never had a job that pays minimum wage.
6. To my knowledge, I have never been discriminated against because of my age, gender, sexual-orientation, or race.

7. I have never been asked to do anything illegal or clearly immoral at work.
8. When not in school, I have never had a gap in employment where I needed to find a job.
9. All my bosses have been good people who did their best to treat those they supervised with respect. A few have even become friends or trusted mentors.
10. Most often, I have found my work to be rewarding and a source of meaning and purpose in my life.

This is not to say my work has always been easy, but it has been privileged.

I have had difficult experiences and situations at work, but I have never had a bad job. One of the first things Ben told me is that when his alarm goes off in the morning, he springs out of bed, excited about the day's work ahead. At the time, I was a year into a new position and I too was excited about my work. But then I ask Ben to tell me about a time he found himself particularly frustrated at work. This is what he said:

> Yeah, I can. In one of the jobs I had, I was working for a trucking company and they basically handled refrigerated loads. There were a handful of really good people there, but there was a lot of turnover at the company. You were pretty much expected to say or do whatever it took to get the load delivered. You had to say or do things which you didn't exactly believe in or knew to be true.
>
> For instance, if a driver agreed to take a load from point A to point B, they might say to you, "Well, can you get me a load coming back this way?" To get the driver to take the load, you'd say, "Oh, yeah, I can do that for you." But you may not really have that load, so the driver gets there, and they make the delivery and say, "Where's my load for the return?" I say, "Oh, sorry, man, somebody else

*took it, or I don't have it anymore." So you had to go on
the limb like that to have people take the load even if that
meant lying to them along the way.*

***

How does the character or quality of our work itself matter?

This is one of those questions that theologians have been
asking for a long time. Another way to ask this question is
to wonder whether some work is itself *good* work. Or is it
the person doing the work that makes it basically good or
bad work?

Remember, the vocational script assumes that all work has the
potential to collaborate with God's work in the world. That's why
the vocational script can slip into the assertation that we should
all understand our work this way.

This very question is one that Martin Luther himself
took on. He took up a version of this question because he
met a man named Assa von Kram, who was a counselor to
a nobleman and a professional solider. Von Kram had asked
Luther whether or not a Christian could also be a soldier,
since their work demanded that they kill others. Von Kram
was so impressed by Luther's response that he encouraged him
to publish his thoughts on the topic so that other soldiers,
too, might benefit.

In 1526, Luther published a pamphlet called "Whether
Soldiers, Too, Can Be Saved." One of the major points he
makes is that some work can be good and right, but that won't
matter much if the work is done by someone who has evil
intentions. Luther goes on to say there is a place in society
for soldiers, because there is a need to protect and defend the
innocent and there is a need to punish those who want to seize
power for themselves by waging war. He admits that war can
be, and is often, horrible—filled with "stabbing and killing,

robbing and burning."[3] That's why it matters who is doing such work. How and why one soldiers is the most important question for Luther.

I was already familiar with this little pamphlet when Ben shared his story with me about working at the trucking company. He clearly didn't think his work there was a calling. In fact, it was one of the worst jobs he had ever had. Revisiting Luther's writings after my time with Ben, however, I was surprised when I read a little more closely. Luther wrote that good work can be corrupted by the person doing the work.

That makes sense.

What Luther doesn't address there, however, is whether bad work can be redeemed by a good worker—someone like Ben. He is one of the kindest people you will ever meet, which is why he just couldn't stomach constantly lying to his colleagues. The "at any cost" work culture required Ben to manipulate and deceive others; it was a requirement of the job, practically a company policy. Like many others before him, he left that job as soon as he could.

I'm glad Ben got out of there, but the question remains: *Can a job that asks you to constantly deceive your colleagues in the name of maximizing profits ever be a vocation?*

I can't know for sure, but I suspect many jobs are a real mixed bag. Ultimately, they provide a tangible material good or service to others, and yet the way the company or organization accomplishes that comes with real costs. Perhaps they cut corners to the detriment of the environment. Or perhaps they are willing to accept high turnover rates as a consequence of their toxic workplace culture. Or perhaps the whole operation depends on the willingness of individual workers to break the law.

Participation in the world of work today requires everyday workers to judge for themselves whether or not their work is

---

3   Martin Luther, "Whether Soldiers Too, Can Be Saved" in *Luther's Works*, American ed., vol. 46, Robert C. Schultz ed. (Philadelphia: Fortress, 1967), 95. Hereafter LW 46.

inherently good, bad, or a mixed bag. Luther probably couldn't have imagined such a world, but he did recognize how complicated this is. At one point in that little pamphlet, he admits that it is just not possible to come up with any hard-and-fast rules for determining whether or not a specific occupation is "good" or "bad."[4] There are just too many exceptions and variables at play.

That, too, makes sense.

But it does raise another question for me. During my interviews with these workers, at some point I would always ask whether or not their Christian faith ever came up at work. For some it did, and for others it rarely—if ever—did. I also asked whether or not their work and the actual challenges they faced there ever came up at church.

None one I interviewed could ever remember that happening.

If there is a relationship between our work and God's, how come our daily work doesn't come up very often at church?

The Micromanager

James, a city planner and engineer, definitely understands his work as a calling. Working for the city government, he understands himself and all his colleagues as public servants. They spend days on master plans and revitalization projects meant to make the city more livable, more economically attractive, and more beautiful. It's easy to see why they would think of their work as a calling to serve the community. Plus, the pastor of the church James

---

4 LW 46:100.

attends regularly talks about vocation and how the whole point of Christian faith is to serve others—especially those in need.

So an open and shut case, right? As long as he understands it that way, what else is there?

That is actually what I used to think about the usefulness of vocational theology. I thought that the whole purpose was to help everyday people of faith connect their work to God's work in the world. But James shared a story with me about his boss that, again, challenged this simplistic way of thinking about our callings.

***

Once, I gave a presentation for the warehouse district and the management team, including the city manager, to give an update. Talked about the different things, different challenges that we were facing in the project, and I had pictures of things that we'd come across and showed it to the group.

Afterwards, I got summoned to the state manager's office and a colleague says, "You better just be careful in there," he said, "This is not good."

And I got pulled into his office and I got my ass reamed for what I had said and what I had talked about because the city manager hadn't been told about whatever it was that I had found or what was seen. That was not a good day. I felt very . . . I just was very . . . I was very angry about how my professional judgment was being questioned when, in my opinion, I thought I was being micromanaged in that particular situation.

The city manager is a very smart individual, but he doesn't have the initials of P.E. (Professional Engineer) after his name. So it was my call on some of the things that we had done in the field; we were making judgment decisions daily. And I was having weekly or bi-weekly meetings with all the owners and keeping them up to speed and letting them know what's going on, and all this information was being documented in minutes and being shared with the city manager, and he didn't read them. So he felt like he was being blindsided.

I made it clear to him. I said, "We've been sharing all this information in minutes." But, yeah, he was pissed. Anyway, from that point forward, he made it real clear. He made the rules of engagement understood: when I come across stuff like that, he is to be notified. He wants to be kept in the loop about everything.

Sometimes he micromanages his departments. And it hurts people.

***

James's story about a boss whose actions leave a wake of hurt behind him stuck with me because it reminded me of a time years ago when I watched a colleague, a supervisor of a department, decimate the self-confidence of everyone who worked for him. He wasn't my boss, but I was close with several others he supervised. He was such a bad supervisor that others had to spend a considerable amount of time offering care and support to colleagues so they could make it another day or week at the office.

Most people didn't make it very long.

In departmental meetings, this supervisor would single out certain people for criticism in front of the whole team. When there were reasons others outside of the department might ask questions or raise criticisms, he would get the team together to "make sure everyone was on the same team." This usually meant some kind of veiled threat if others said too much about what was really going on. He was a master at gaslighting those around him.

This particular supervisor was especially cruel to the women who worked for him. During my short time there, all the women quit. And they were all incredibly talented. A year after one colleague left, she would still tear up at even the mention of the supervisor's name. That's called trauma.

Two years after I left, I still got nearly weekly phone calls from one colleague. I would listen, and we would talk through ways to get by or whether it was time for him to leave the organization. Thankfully, he did eventually get out, and he got a major promotion too.

I know of at least two significant efforts to document this man's tyranny and bring it to the attention of human resources. One senior leader actually said, "Well, let's just slow down. We don't want to ruin anyone's life here." I thought that was especially ironic considering the daily abuse this man was dishing out to others.

To be honest, I don't know if James' boss—the micromanager—was as bad as the supervisor I watched inflict so much pain onto those around me. But when James said that last line, "And it hurts people," I immediately had sympathy for James and his colleagues.

***

I doubt we need theologians to tell us that there are some awful people in powerful positions in the workplace. But what does that have to do with vocation?

The vocational script is a powerful story, one that provides a sense of meaning and purpose across many different types of work. In some situations, having a sense of call provides the motivation to serve others in the midst of challenging circumstances. Here I think about some of the teachers I know who have served in under-resourced school districts or those who travel to disaster zones to provide care in the aftermath of natural disasters. When a sense of calling is invoked in such situations, it is inspiring.

But there is a dark side to the vocational script. At times, the language of vocation can underwrite or justify working conditions that are not just challenging; they are outright abusive, sinful. When conditions cross that line, it matters little whether workers think of their work as callings or not.

If you have a boss who is abusive, you don't have a vocation at work anymore.

Unfortunately, I can be certain that at this very moment, there is someone who is suffering through an abusive work relationship, and they are holding on to that job because they think it is a calling, and that because it is a calling, they must simply endure the abuse.

We need theologians and pastors to start talking about this darker side of vocation.

"I Got Called a Motherf'er One Too Many Times"

When I arrived in Seguin, Texas, in August of 2008, I had a singular purpose for being at Texas Lutheran University: I wanted to become a teacher. I wonder how many people are inspired to become a teacher because of one or two significant teachers in their own lives? Three teachers had inspired me:

Mr. Carter, my first band director—a man whose sheer intensity willed musical excellence into being and often with too few students and fewer resources.

Ms. Allan, my high school English teacher—a woman who set the standards high and wouldn't let us stop until we achieved them; she wrote more on our papers than we did.

Mr. Huie, my second band director—a man whose patience and generosity seemed endless and whose constant encouragement propelled my awkward teenage self toward young adulthood.

I wasn't a bad student in high school, but I wasn't an academic standout either. But that first semester, I was clear about what I wanted. Never had my schooling mattered more.

***

I met Valerie, a teacher and teacher trainer, during one my first weekends of interviewing for my project. Her story was instantly compelling. She had been previously married and had adopted a son. After a divorce, she sought a more stable career and went back to school to become a teacher. She was a hero already in my book.

Valerie's early experiences in the classroom were also inspiring. She had taught at a vocational high school (similar to a technical school), where many of her students would transition from graduation immediately into the workforce. And later she taught at a school in an underserved school district. At the time of the interview, however, she taught in a school district located in one of the state's most wealthy suburbs. It was great to have resources for once, but it also came with an oversized sense of entitlement. A parent's involvement in their child's education is a good thing, but educators are trained professionals. They spend years preparing for a career in education, and many of them have an even deeper well of wisdom dug from the depths of their experience in the classroom. Even so, many parents insist they know best when it comes to their own children's schooling.

I wasn't surprised to learn that early on, Valerie thought of her work as a calling. I was surprised, however, to learn what disabused her of that view.

Some teachers will tell you this is a calling. This is my passion. This is my love. Not for me anymore. And I'm a good teacher.

I mean, I really believe that. I believe I'm a good teacher. But this is not—I'm ready to leave it. I'm ready to find joy again in what I do. I mean the teacher-trainer part. If I had to go back into the classroom, I would never do it. I wouldn't go back, which is really sad. There's a lot of teachers who feel like I do—especially teachers my age. They've seen a dynamic change in education, and they just don't want anything to do with it anymore.

Public education is tricky business. For those who commit their lives to it, their life's work is one of public service, investing in the lives of young people on their way to (hopefully) becoming contributing members of society. Yet, with public funding comes public accountability and involvement. Valerie was starting to see how the relationship between educators and the public they served was starting to crack:

Teachers have somehow become the bane of society. I would never ever encourage my child to become a teacher anymore which is really, really sad. We are supposed to solve all of society's ills. Then when we do that, we get told, on the other hand, why are you interfering in my parenting? That's up to me as the parent or me as the church or whatever. So we get blamed for everything. We're held out to be incompetent and that we don't know what we're doing. That somehow, we just stand around all day long and want kids to fail. And then on top of it, there is no home discipline left anymore. So children feel entitled and bold to act, say, treat you in any way that they want to. And there's very little you can do about it. I got called a motherfucker one too many times.

***

Valerie's story is a classic example of what happens when the vocational script collapses. There was a time when that script was a plausible account of her working life. But over time, conditions "on the ground" became too much. All work is a daily grind, and teaching is especially so. Valerie seems to have experienced something altogether different. What Valerie is talking about is not simply a tough day or a tough week at work. She's describing what can happen when conditions at work are so bad that one loses one's sense of meaning and purpose there.

Valerie had difficulty thinking of her work as a calling because certainly God would not call her to a place where her gifts are ignored, where the very people she serves despise her, and the students in her classroom verbally abuse her. None of that sounds like it would have anything to do with God's work in the world. I have to agree with Valerie; that doesn't sound like God's desire for her or anyone else.

I'm afraid understanding the potential for one's work to be a calling simply isn't enough. It isn't enough because many jobs have challenges that are beyond our control. These "structural constraints," as I call them, can make otherwise important work seem like just a job. Or worse, they can transform the work into something destructive.

L. Callid Keefe-Perry, a theologian and scholar of education, has written about the destructive tension present for many teachers today. Keefe-Perry writes that teachers today often find themselves in a "crucible"—stuck between a powerful narrative that says their work is a calling and a concrete reality where policies and regulations violate the very motivations that led them into education. He writes,

> Because so many teachers conceive of their profession as vocation, the challenges of the job, and their struggles with success are experienced dually as both professionally and spiritually difficult. Furthermore, there is a binding that

catches at the intersection of a personal sense of vocation and structural dynamics that challenges the ability of teachers to live into that call with integrity [. . .] The teaching profession is a crucible in which one's sense of call is tested, and the heat is rising.[5]

What scholars like Keefe-Perry and practitioners on the ground like Valerie know is that the vocational script is deeply problematic in education today, despite its popularity. It might be tempting to resolve this tension by calling out the idealized intentions teachers may have. Perhaps teacher-training programs should let them know beforehand what they're really in for.

Unfortunately, the situation is beyond simplistic resolutions. *How do we transform the educational system to prioritize the dignity of teachers? How do we convince an entire society that educators and parents are on the same team? And how do we create career pathways that will encourage the best and the brightest to enter a profession that has such a formative role in our nation's youth?*

Perhaps the situation on the ground is different for some, but until we answer big societal questions like these, for many, teaching will continue to be an anti-vocation, a job that doesn't "bring life abundant" as the Scriptures say, but one that afflicts moral injury on teachers.

***

I don't know if Mr. Carter, Ms. Allan, or Mr. Huie ever thought about their work as a calling, or if they, too, were called motherfuckers. What I do know is that I was not the only student they inspired. The thought that there's a chance they were treated like Valerie makes me sick.

---

5 L. Callid Keefe-Perry, "Called into Crucible: Vocation and Moral Injury in U.S. Public School Teachers," *Religious Education* 113 (2018), 494.

I was very close to becoming a teacher, and for a while, I thought that was my calling. Listening to Valerie and other teachers in my research left me with something like survivor's guilt. The winding path that led to becoming a professional theologian only makes things worse. The seminary classroom is not, thankfully, much like a public-school classroom. If it were, I'm sure I would not last nearly long as Valerie.

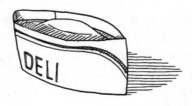

Corporate "Ethics"

During college, I worked briefly for a coffee shop, and I got to know the owners well—Terry, Jill, Jerry, and Donna—so when they asked if I wanted to work a few shifts, it was an easy "yes!" It wasn't just a coffee shop, actually. It was also a chiropractor's practice. Terry, the chiropractor, had carved out a private office where he could see his patients. Just outside that office was a small desk where a receptionist would welcome patients and take their payments. Sometimes I'd work the desk and sometimes I'd pull shots of espresso.

On the wall opposite of the reception desk was a set of shelves filled with a curated selection of books on Christian spirituality. Books by Richard Rohr, a Catholic writer, were especially prominent. As I got to know the owners, I learned that all four were Lutheran—though Terry and Jill went to one Lutheran church and Jerry and Donna went to another. All four were quite involved in the local community. Over time, my relationship with them deepened and I began to think of them more as mentors and surrogate parents than bosses.

At the beginning of my senior year of college, through a series of events, a group of friends and I started a church, and the coffee shop became a key place for our gatherings. The owners even let us keep the place open late on Thursday nights. The church's leadership was made up entirely of young adults and as we began to organize ourselves, it was clear we needed some adults in the room. So we created two groups—a board of directors to help manage our organizational life and a council of elders to add some deeper wisdom into the mix. Donna agreed to serve on the board while Terry and Jill served as elders.

That coffee shop was a hub of community and hospitality. It needed to make money, but its real purpose was a gift to the town. The owners created that place because they believed their community needed a "third place," as sociologist Ray Oldenburg called them.[6] In Oldenburg's thinking, third places are unique places that serve a special role in our society. Third places have several distinct characteristics:

They are leveling places. That is, they are places where it doesn't matter where you come from—whether you're well-off or living on the margins. Anyone could pop in for a cup of coffee.

They are places for conversation. If you wanted a quiet place to study, you probably didn't go to the coffee shop. But if you wanted a lively place where you might get swept away into a conversation with regulars, it was the place to be.

They are hospitable places. Like all third places, the coffee shop went out of its way to be accessible and accommodating to everyone who walked through the doors.

They have regulars. If I wandered into the coffee shop in the morning, the staff knew what I would be drinking. If I came for lunch, my order was ready by the time I got to the front of the line. And that was true for all of us regulars.

---

6 Ray Oldenburg, *The Great Good Place: Cafes, Coffee Shops, Bookstores, Bars, Hair Salons, and Other Hangouts at the Heart of a Community* (Cambridge, MA: Da Capo Press, 1999), xvii.

They are homes away from home. Typically, third places are unpretentious; they have a homey feel to them that makes them a home away from home. At the coffee shop, sofas were as numerous as tables for sitting. The shop was like a large public living room.

They are playful places. Donna is the most hospitable person I know. When someone walked in the door, they'd often get a loud greeting from across the shop. Her hair and fingernails were as loud as her personality, and they were always fun. She was the soul of that coffee shop.

Even though I knew the owners to be people of deep faith, even though the place was shaped by their own Christian values of hospitality and community, even though it had that whole book section of Christian spirituality, and even though our church frequently set up shop there, it was not a "Christian" coffee shop. Describing it that way would be too small for its wide embrace. It was just a coffee shop—a really good coffee shop.

***

As a researcher, I am probably not supposed to have favorite research subjects. I'm sure many would say it is better for us to have a certain amount of emotional distance from those we observe and interview. Having favorites could be undesirable; it's like having a favorite child.

Still, John is one of my favorites. His authenticity was captivating. But the more I read his interviews and listened to his audio journals, I began to wonder if his authenticity was creating problems at work for him. He had a sense of integrity that he expected of himself and of others. Problem was, his CEO didn't share John's sense of integrity. Because John knew his CEO belonged to a church and considered himself a Christian, this bothered him. It bothered him a lot:

Recently I've been trying to understand the ethics of the corporation because it is driven by personalities, how the corporation ends up doing some of the things it does. What happened was there was a recall at a company that was making a product for us—and they did their sole business through us—but the personalities of their owner and our CEO clashed. [The vendor] had a great relationship with the former CEO, but now these two people despise each other.

It was almost like [the CEO] was trying to make a point that [the vendor] was going to fail. He didn't want them to do any more of our business, and they did nothing wrong. It was all on a personal level. It's still hard to stay out of the middle of it because I feel strongly what our corporation did was wrong. And now it's in litigation, so I will probably be in the middle of that doing some depositions.

By the time John was recording audio journals for me, lawyers had gotten involved, and the pressure of the legal proceedings had been weighing on him. Sometimes John would record his audio journals in the car. At one point, he pulled over and recorded this:

Please, God, help. In any way you can, help me understand why this is all happening. Let alone help these people. I pray that God just shows us and is with all those people that are involved in this, that he helps comfort them and that they know God is there to help them through this.

***

John's story raises an important question for me. How do Christians behave or react at work? If Christianity makes a difference in our everyday lives, certainly it should make a difference in the way we treat people at work. I think John is right; it should make a difference.

It makes sense to me that we Christians would *want* our faith to shape our working lives. The easy way out here is to conclude that the CEO isn't a Christian after all; he's not a *real* Christian. But if I'm honest, I suspect either that is too simplistic, or Christianity just doesn't have that kind of impact. I have little doubt John is a real Christian, but any difference he might have made was muted by the lawyers' non-disclosure agreements and no-contact orders.

Sometimes being a Christian just isn't enough to overcome the evil and sin we encounter daily at work. That is not a commentary on the church, just a confession of our need for God's work in the world.

Your kingdom come, your will be done; on earth as it is in heaven.

***

About a year into working at the coffee shop, I was managing the Thursday night shift, trying to finish college, had already begun graduate studies, and there was the church we were starting. One day, Terry, Jill, Donna, and Jerry sat me down and explained in no uncertain terms that I was in over my head, and that the business was suffering because of it. Donna named all the things on my plate, and then asked, "Do you want to keep doing this? It's okay if you don't."

Even as a twenty-year old who thought I was invincible, I knew they were right. We came up with a plan and a few weeks later I ended my time working for the coffee shop. Whether that was the Christian thing to do, or just the right decision for the business, I don't know. I'm not even sure that matters.

Lonely at the Top

Higher education is a strange field. In some ways, it is shaped by forces just like any other business. Customers, competition, marketing, talent retention, government regulation, and the like shape the present and future of the field. In other ways, however, higher education is shaped by its long history going back to the medieval era when the earliest universities appeared in places such as Bologna, Oxford, Cambridge, and Paris.

Back then, universities were made up of self-organized scholars who were recognized by civil and/or church authorities. Faculties were organized by discipline (i.e., the Faculty of Law or the Faculty of Medicine) and eventually combined to form colleges and universities. Originally, the very name *college* or *university* referred not to the place of study, but to group of scholars who offered lectures and tutorials. The faculty *was* the university.

If higher education is a strange field, theological education is even stranger. Theologians, along with scholars of law and medicine, were among the earliest faculties to organize themselves into colleges and universities; we're especially proud of that fact. Today, some theologians continue to teach in university-affiliated divinity schools and graduate schools of theology, but many of us teach in small, independent, church-affiliated schools. These seminaries have to compete with their university-affiliated peers, but with a fraction of the resources.

Whether working at a divinity school or a seminary, theologians go to work in institutions shaped by ancient traditions and modern economic forces. Early on in my career, I learned that those ancient traditions are alive and well. Some of these traditions are just part of the pomp and circumstance of it all, like the multi-colored robes faculty wear at graduations. Other traditions, such as faculty status and rank, painfully matter—as I learned the hard way.

Early on in my career, I was working at a seminary while finishing up my dissertation. It was a new position, one that was originally imagined as an administrative position, but since I had taught at the school before and because I would continue to offer courses, I was granted faculty "status." This meant that officially I was a member of the faculty (I had "voice" but no vote to get technical). Because I had not yet finished my doctorate, I was given the rank of "instructor."

When I arrived at the school, I was eager to keep making progress on my dissertation, so I paid a visit to the library to ask about acquiring a library card. The librarian at the circulation desk referred me to the head librarian.

"Hi, I'm Tim. How can I check out books and how long can I keep them? I'm working on my dissertation and there's a good number of books I will need."

"Oh, well staff don't have library privileges, only faculty do."

"Well, good thing, I'm faculty."

"No, you're not. You're staff."

"Right, and faculty.

"No, you're staff."

"No, really I'm faculty—I am an instructor."

"You'll have to talk to the dean."

I did just that, and soon I was back in the library getting everything I needed. It turned out to be a silly thing, but it was the first of many instances where I was reminded that I was at the bottom of the academic ladder and that my faculty status was a second-class citizenship.

Episodes like this would happen often. Ironically, the one place on campus that wasn't confused about my role was my classroom. My students didn't care much about the politics around my faculty status or what rank I held. They were blissfully ignorant of all this. To them, I must be their professor because I was the one giving the grades.

***

I had heard enough stories from others in the field to expect some of the academic hazing I experienced, so I mostly shrugged it off—even if it did bother me. But the real impact of it became clear in a conversation with Mitch, the accidental banker.

As Mitch climbed the ranks at the bank, he spent less time reviewing loans and instead spent more time building the team around him. The college basketball star knew a thing or two about working together as a team. A big part of his job is to lead the managers who are responsible for hiring and developing the team. The kind of investment he spends the most time on is the investment the bank makes in its employees.

Mitch's passion for investing in new staff made me wonder if I should put in an application. Here's how he put it in his own words:

> *I was telling my wife this just the other day. We've experienced a lot of change in [nearby metro area] but had an opportunity to spend some time with the team and it was just fun. There's just something that youth brings. Inexperience and that kind of thing, but it also brings an energy that's contagious. I told my wife, 'It's been a long time since I was that excited about that group.' Just the makeup and the chemistry that's there. Time will tell if that delivers the way I think it will. But*

when you're building talent and selecting talent, you have to be incredibly patient because it's too easy to fall into a practice of 'just fill the warm seat because you have to.' You've got to have some things get done, and you can make some short-term decisions that are not really good long term. Sometimes it takes a little coercion to get them to understand that that is their best interest long term.

I was taken aback by the excitement in his voice as he talked about this new, young group of employees. But I was taken aback even more by what he said in response to a question about times he's found his work frustrating. He said:

In my position, at my level, you look around the room and go, who do I talk to? There's not many. When you're not getting [mentored] in the way you're being asked to mentor others that's probably the most frustrating part. Because I think there are probably some things I could have done that I would have liked to do. But you need some sponsorship.

Mitch spends much of his time investing in others. Once you get to his position at the top, however, it's rather lonely. No one invests in Mitch anymore.

***

Often workers today are described as individualistic. There is this idea that when it comes to work and the economy, we are all basically selfish—that what most people care about is themselves. What matters most is what benefits me, myself, and I.

I suppose there is a fair amount of that in the world of work today. But it is also true that, perhaps more than ever, success at work requires others. We need each other at work more than ever because many jobs are highly specialized and require collaboration. Those at the bottom need those above them to take an interest in them and their success. Those at the top need those under them to grow into the best version of themselves possible. No matter where your job fits on the organizational chart, you need peers because very little work today can be done alone.

As a theologian, I find this to be incredible. The more complex our social world, the more we need each other, the more interdependent we become. We may recognize that or not. We may step up to that reality or fall short. Having listened to so many stories from work, there are many things about the nature of the working world that I would not want to attribute to God. However, I might be willing to concede that God is behind our growing interdependence. If Gustav Wingren were writing on vocation today, perhaps he would say, "God doesn't need your good works, but your colleague at work does—more than ever."[7]

***

"But you need some sponsorship."

That was the line that got me. In that moment, it was as if Mitch was talking directly to me. It was as if we had switched places, and he was the one listening to me tell stories about *my* work. Of course, he knew nothing about the strange faculty politics I was encountering. To me those five words about his loneliness at top were a revelation for me. What was true for Mitch at

---

7 In the original quote, Wingren writes, "God does not need your good works, but your neighbor does." See *Gustav Wingren, Luther on Vocation* (Eugene, OR: Wipf and Stock, reprint 2004), 10.

the bank was true for me at the seminary. I needed sponsorship, and I didn't have it. If that didn't change, I would be stuck in professional purgatory.

Retaliation

The process of becoming a pastor in my Lutheran tradition is complicated. It includes a course of study like many other professions, but it also includes things like psychological screenings, extensive background checks, clinical work usually in a hospital, a series of meetings and retreats with a regional committee that oversees the process, and more paperwork than I had expected. Still, I enjoyed the process.

I began the process when I was working to start a church. That, too, was surprising to me. Because we were starting the church within the Lutheran tradition, the local bishop and his staff were involved. There is no way I would have started down the path to become a pastor were it not for that faith community. The truth is I didn't feel a sense of call to be the pastor of a typical Lutheran church, but the creativity of the community I served gave me hope that a new kind of church was possible. If a church like that wanted me to be their pastor, I was up for that.

In my twenties, I had a bad habit of getting in over my head. I did it working at the coffee shop, and I did it later on with the new church. So when the bishop suggested I focus my energy on my theological studies instead of trying to juggle full-time work and full-time study, I knew that was the right thing to do. Leaving that community behind was one of the hardest things I had done.

Not long after I arrived on campus in St. Paul, Minnesota, I received a note from a friend and colleague still working for the new church. The bishop was pulling the funding; without those resources, there was little hope the church could go on. A group of people rallied and wrote a letter pleading with the bishop to reverse course, but no amount of advocacy was going to change the situation.

Personally, this was devastating news, but it also presented me with a professional dilemma. The committee that oversees the process of becoming a pastor is, in a sense, an extension of the bishop's ministry. In a few months, I would be at a retreat, and inevitably they would ask, "So how's it going?" As far as I could tell, I had two options. I could lie and say everything was fine, that I was learning so much and looking forward to next steps. Or I could tell the truth that the bishop's actions had given me real doubts about what I was doing. Neither seemed like good options, so I reluctantly withdrew from the process and began a season of soul-searching.

***

I was not surprised to learn that Valerie, the teacher trainer, was involved in the teacher's association. She was clearly passionate about helping other teachers, so it seemed pretty logical that she would find her way to leadership in the organization that advocated on behalf of teachers. I'm not sure why, but I never could have guessed how political a teacher's association could be. Here's a story she told me about an episode of retaliation—one that continues to bring her pain years later:

I have served as the president of the teacher's association—twice in this district. I have worked with all of the teachers in the district. We have about 450 members in the association, and it has been very fulfilling to me to be able to help people who feel like they didn't have a voice. They didn't understand a path forward. They didn't know how to navigate the system. They didn't know the questions to ask. They didn't know what their rights were. Sometimes that means helping teachers who shouldn't be teachers figure out that maybe they needed to find a different career path. But I think I was pretty successful at that. I had to develop some relationships with our superintendent, the district head of HR. I had to learn how to have very difficult conversations with them and also with teachers. I did find a great deal of satisfaction that many people said to me, "I could never have done this. Thank you for standing by me. Thank you for helping me through this. Thank you for being there. I wouldn't have known what to do if somebody hadn't helped me to do this."

Because her advocacy role occasionally means confronting administrators, she has, at times, found herself on the receiving end of their retribution.

Probably the worst time for me was moving to this district. My first couple of years here were pretty good. I got along okay with my principal. But then I got heavily involved in the association, and there were problems at the high school where I taught. The principal decided that she could not keep my work up with the association separated from my work as a teacher. And she started making my teaching unbearable; she made my job extremely difficult to the point that one year when I left school at the end of the school year,

I had no classes assigned to me in the fall. I had a teaching contract, but I had no classes. Zero. I did not have classes assigned to me until five days before school started. I didn't know what I was going to be teaching in the fall. Then because of that, it just escalated. The state association had to get involved. It was horrible. It got quite nasty. From that time on until the time she retired, it was a very difficult working situation.

***

I have a lot of sympathy for Valerie and her predicament. One of the key theological claims of the Christian tradition is that God forgives us while we are still sinners. To put that another way, God offers us grace unconditionally; there is not a series of steps for us to take before God is willing to grant us grace. Of course, forgiveness and healing between two (or more) people is quite a bit more complicated.

A few years ago, I learned that there are social scientists who research forgiveness. When I learned that, I immediately thought it was incredible. There's a lot of research where its application is difficult to understand, but forgiveness research sounded endlessly useful.

Clinical psychologist and researcher Steven Sandage has developed a three-phase model for interpersonal forgiveness.[8] The model begins with the psychological and spiritual practice of lament—actually facing the pain caused by the conflict between people. As it turns out, we often need others to help us find the empathy we need to acknowledge our own disappointment,

---

8 Steven J. Sandage and F. LeRon Shults, *The Faces of Forgiveness: Searching for Wholeness and Salvation* (Grand Rapids: Baker Publishing, 2003), 91–99.

anger, and shame. The second phase encourages empathy and humility. Empathy, like compassion, is the capacity to acknowledge the suffering or limits of our offenders. Extending empathy need not absolve responsibility, but it serves an important role in allowing us to see them in a fuller context. The humility part comes in when we recognize we, too, are capable of harming others.

Just as we tell ourselves, and others, stories about the meaning of our work, we also tell such stories about the relationships we encounter. In fact, how we understand ourselves is also connected to the stories we tell. That's why Sandage includes the practice of extending "narrative horizons" as his third phase of forgiveness. What Sandage has in mind here is coming to view forgiveness as a theme of a larger story we tell about our lives, as a strategy of sorts for coping with our interpersonal conflicts. When we get stuck in these conflicts, forgiveness can be a way of moving toward growth. If possible, forgiveness can also help us regain a sense of hope for the future—either our own future or the future of a relationship.

For two years, I had the joy of being Steven Sandage's teaching assistant. I learned more about practicing empathy and forgiveness during those two years than I did in a lifetime of participation in the church. That seems unfortunate. I wonder if that would be different if our churches were places where we actually shared stories like the one Valerie shared with me. If such storytelling was a more regular part of congregational life, I wonder if we would discover practices that might help us cope with the darker side of our working lives—practices like forgiveness.

***

Just as Valerie experienced ongoing pain and anger with her principal, I was really angry at that bishop. I experienced his invitation to pursue full-time study, and his decision to terminate the funding of a community that meant so much to me left me feeling betrayed and duped into leaving for the seminary. When I tell the story of how I became a theologian, I don't usually tell this part of the story. I'd rather not revisit it. On the other hand, maybe I need to extend my "narrative horizons," as Steve would say.

5

Harvest

Despite the toll it takes, there is meaning and purpose in our working lives. The stories that follow demonstrate as much; however, they may surprise you.

Theologians in the twentieth century have often assumed that much of what we experience in our so-called "secular" lives is misguided, or worse, meaningless. They survey the public narratives of advertising and the latest headlines about corporate greed and conclude that consumerism is a thin substitute for the purpose of our lives. These narratives may animate economic life, but they offer nothing for the workers who are sacrificed on the altar of capitalism. It is a rather bleak assessment of contemporary work—a place most of us give incredible time and energy.

I do not disagree with their social analysis, but I heard very little in the stories of everyday work that resonated with it. It seems theologians and ordinary workers are speaking right past each other; it is as if the two are engaged in two entirely separate conversations. What I hear is not that work is meaningless, but that there are *so many* ways to think about the meaning of work, that it is difficult to weave them all together into a single story. In fact, that is one of the most significant insights I learned from these workers: *no single story can capture the meaning and purpose of contemporary work.*

Harvesting these stories for their sense of meaning and purpose reveals a rather diverse set of crops. For some, the meaning of work is found in the work itself, in the process of it and the task at hand. For others, what matters is that the work makes a difference in their local communities or beyond. Many say it is the opportunity for personal growth that brings a sense of purpose to the work. Several told stories about the people they met at work and how meaningful those relationships became. Though it may come as a surprise, a few even told stories about the care and solidarity they experienced at work. And nearly all these workers had something to say about the legacy of their work—what they hoped mattered in the end.

In order to hear these stories *theologically*, it is helpful to think about these stories in two very different ways. Some of these stories speak to a *transcendent* God at work. Here I do not mean "transcendence" in its typical sense—as a way of naming God's existence beyond the physical, material world. Rather, I simply mean that some of these stories point beyond work itself. They present as stories about work, but they are ultimately stories about something else altogether: the common good, human existence, and the like. Transcendence in this sense implies that God is at work in those stories. Other stories, however, speak to an *immanent* God. Here I mean that God is directly involved within the work, as if the workers themselves become the face of God or God's own hands and feet in the world.

What is most surprising however is that the stories that follow remain narratives about the daily grind of work. It is within this daily grind that we hear how workers understand the ultimate meanings of their working lives.

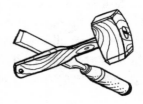

Crafting Caskets

I never have been able to work from home. As a teenager, I would go with friends to a Starbucks to study. In college, I did most of my work in the practice rooms of the music department, but when I needed to read or write a paper, I usually went to the library or to the coffee shop/chiropractor's office. The same was true throughout my graduate studies. For a short time, I was lucky to work for a professor who had three offices—one for each of the various hats she wore. She was kind enough to get me a key to one of her offices, and I set up shop there as often as I could.

In 2019, when the COVID-19 pandemic hit, my wife and I were living in a six -hundred-square-foot apartment. She already worked from home, so like many other people, we suddenly had to learn how to work from our shared space. It was awful. Eventually, we were allowed back into our faculty offices on campus, but very few people were ever there. Except me. I was there occupying what felt like a post-apocalyptic disaster zone. The whole world was a disaster zone. I roamed the unlit hallways like some kind of sentinel guarding an abandoned fortress.

I got used to the lonely nature of it, the deafening silence of the large empty lecture halls and the shuttered library. Each day, I would come in, work, eat lunch at my desk, and then go home again. I felt slightly guilty because this arrangement suited me quite well and I was extraordinarily productive.

***

As I got used to my new solitary existence at work, I remembered that some people, like Ben, worked this way even before the pandemic. Each day when his alarm went off, he popped right out of bed. Or that's what he told me. He really liked his job working alongside the brothers of a religious order making caskets and urns in their workshop. The monks had signed up for a simple life of work and prayer. Ben hadn't taken vows, but he enjoyed the monastic nature of his job. It was part of what he found most meaningful about his work.

At my invitation, Ben recorded a series of audio journals reflecting on his daily work among the monks. This one below is representative of what he recorded each day over about two weeks:

> *Work today was pretty good. It was short. Five-hour day today, and I worked on what's called face-framing. That's putting together the pieces to form the sides of the casket, and so that's what I did today. I made the sides for six walnut caskets, and then I ran them through the sander, and then these pieces are taken over and they're put together by other people. And when they're put together, they go over to finish sanding, and we progress through the system until [the pieces are] a finished product.*
>
> *One thing nice about that [is that] it's a solitary job, so you work by yourself—you have time to think or not think. Since I work in what I consider a holy place, it gives me time to think about God and his direction in my life and to thank him for the current job I have because I really do enjoy it.*

No one in my research study said they enjoyed their work as often as Ben did. Nearly every day during those two weeks, he shared with me his gratitude that he got to work in a special place, a "holy place" even, where his faith and his skills come together. I'm sure it was quite a contrast after working at the trucking company, where he was always lying to his colleagues about return shipments. For Ben, the chance to practice his faith openly at work was a massive fringe benefit.

> *A lot of places, if you talk about your faith, they look at you funny, but where I work, it's a big plus. You can talk about your faith and share your faith. I do enjoy that.*

There are intangibles in a job. Sure, you can get your wages, your insurance, holidays, and vacation time, but there are many other intangibles when it comes to choosing a job. I'm sure if I chose to, I could get a sales job making probably twice as much money, but I don't care for that. I don't need that anymore. I enjoy what I do and the place where I work. It is a blessing where I work, and not many people can say that where they work is a blessing.

***

What Ben is saying here is really quite interesting. He is not simply saying that he has a good job (although he says that too—all the time!). In fact, he is discounting many of the very things that would cause others to claim as much. Other jobs may have their own unique "intangibles," as Ben calls them, but he is willing to stay in a job that admittedly does not pay very well, precisely because of its intangibles. Ben named many of those intangibles: the solitary, quiet work; opportunities to talk to others about his faith; using a range of his people skills; and the relaxed approach to taking time off. He goes much further than saying it's a "good job": he uses explicitly theological language, calling it a *blessing*.

I have to admit that I did not ever ask Ben what, exactly, he meant by calling his work a "blessing." While he was the only one who said the job itself was the blessing, other participants used the word in a different way. They spoke of the many blessings their work provided: large homes in the suburbs, college educations for their children, or the family vacations. In this sense, living a "good life" was akin to "being blessed." But it is clear that Ben could not have meant *that* because his job at the monastery provided only a very modest income.

Christian Scharen, a New York City-based theologian and pastor, has written about the way we Americans have transformed the whole idea of a blessing into something that is fundamentally *ours*. It has become a way to shine the spotlight on our privileges. Yet Scharen goes on to remind us that the original biblical logic of a blessing includes a tension—it is both a privilege *and a responsibility*. Drawing on Scripture's paradigmatic example, Scharen reminds us that though Abraham was indeed blessed with children in his old age, the entire purpose of that gift from God is so that Abraham himself (and his offspring!) will become a blessing. In this way, Scharen writes, all blessings link what we have been given to the needs of others.[1]

Ben might not have put it quite like Scharen did, but I got the sense that he understood that the meaning of his work was not, and actually could not, be found in what it materially provided him. Rather, it was found between solitary work and offering daily hospitality. He certainly had a different kind of blessing in mind.

✳✳✳

I also have to admit that I have mostly thought of those solitary pandemic days as a privilege. After all, I have a job that allowed me to shelter myself from a death-dealing pandemic. Now that those days are mostly behind us, Ben and Scharen are messing with how I understand my own work. I have never not seen it as a privilege, but a responsibility, a gift that tethers my daily work to the needs of others. I could work on that.

---

1 Christian Scharen, "Blessing," in *The Wiley-Blackwell Companion to Practical Theology*, Bonnie J. Miller-McLemore, ed. (Malden, MA: Wiley-Blackwell Publishers, 2012), 85.

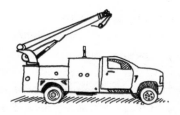

"Best Thing I Ever Did"

Perhaps you have never thought about this, but a lot of jobs in the church are dead-end jobs.

For example, I was worked as Director of Education at a church for five hours a week. The position paid about $5,000 annually at the time and included no benefits whatsoever. Now I took the job during a season of life when a very part-time position made sense for me. I wanted to be involved in ministry, but I had another full-time job, so I could not have accepted anything other than a position like this one.

As far as church work goes, this is fairly common.

Think about how often churches create part-time positions with no benefits.

Think about how often churches create positions because other staff don't want to do that part of ministry.

Think about how often churches create positions that have no upward career path.

Having served for a decade in congregational ministry, I know exactly why this happens and I do not mean to suggest that there are not good reasons why these positions exist. And I know that many people find these positions to be significant opportunities to share their gifts with the church in ways that we cannot easily duplicate with volunteers. I know! I get it.

Still, as far as jobs go, many of these positions really are not great.

Once I was teaching a seminary course, and I invited my students to spend ten minutes describing their dream first position as a pastor. As they took turns sharing what they had written, one young man half-heartedly described a small, struggling church with no youth or children and no real sense of purpose. The tone of his voice suggested that this was less his dream and more what he expected. When I asked him about this, he said, "Well, we all have to put in our time."

Ouch, I thought.

He went on to say that, in his tradition, early career pastors usually ended up at churches like this, and that he was worried about how he would support his family of four. He had spent a few years in the business world before beginning seminary and was surprised when denominational leaders (veteran pastors) told him that it would be inappropriate to try to negotiate the salary package offered by a church. He should be thankful for whatever compensation they could afford.

Double ouch, I thought.

***

Both that student and that five-hour-per-week part-time position came to my mind as I listened to Sally tell her story. When I asked her if she ever thought of her work as a calling, this is how she responded:

Well, maybe.

I'll give you two examples. When I worked at the church, I just thoroughly enjoyed that for the simple fact that I knew so many of the parishioners having grown up in that congregation. They would come and share their issues, their stories. I just felt like I was caring for those folks.

When I decided to look for different employment after the church, we were going through some financial issues out at the farm. The kids [had] graduated and the salary at the church wasn't much, no benefits, the whole nine yards. So I thought, "I'm just going to go look and see what else is out there." And I went to a local employment center, filled out their application, and that's how I got an interview at the natural gas company. Best thing I ever did.

It was a great place to work, great benefits. My starting pay was double . . . what I was making at the church. I was just ready to grow myself personally and they had nothing but all sorts of opportunities for me. When they had training, I would go do it. So I did a lot of traveling.

Later on in our interview, Sally shared with me that eventually she became an operations manager at the utility company. Here's how she described what that meant to her:

When I was in the supervisor position, I would take at least two days out of the year and ride with my employees because they were field technicians . . . We built great friendships and relationships—that wasn't always the case in settings like that. But it's amazing today, even when I see them out on the street, they will say, "Give me a hug."

Yeah. So we were quite a family.

One day, when she was recording an audio journal at my invitation, she mentioned that she was headed to a former colleague's retirement party to drop off a gift. That was after the natural gas company eliminated her position during budget cuts! Even then, Sally remained close to her colleague. They really were a family.

Time and again participants in my research told me that it was the relationships they formed at work that mattered most. They mattered because it was through those relationships that they experienced and offered care and support. Work is a daily grind that takes its toll. Often it is the solidarity and support of others that make all the difference.

This is not surprising, but it is countercultural. We ask children what they want to be when they grow up, as if the most important question is what the work itself is or what the status of our work conveys to others. We do not ask them *how* they want to work or what kind of *colleagues* they want to meet or be. The world of work is often described as a dehumanizing one where all that really matters are results and profits. I have no doubt that, for some, work is this way. But it is not the only story we should listen to. We should listen to the workers.

***

A working life is often a very long time. In the United States, the working life is about fifty years on average. That is a long time not to grow. Certainly, God must care about the ways we grow (or not) at work.

Those of us who come from the Lutheran tradition can, at times, struggle with this idea of growth or development. The fancy, technical way to put it is that we have a healthy sense of human finitude. Or, in other words, Luther did not put a whole lot of stock in our ability to overcome sin. He thought that our very human nature was fundamentally corrupt. Perhaps the best way to capture what Luther had in mind is to turn to Paul's letter to the Romans. There, Paul writes:

> I do not understand my own actions. For I do not do what I want, but I do the very thing I hate . . . For I know that nothing good dwells within me, that is, in my flesh. I can will what is right, but I cannot do it. For I do not do the good I want, but the evil I do not want is what I do. (Romans 7:15, 18)

At times, Luther himself used the Latin phrase *incurvatus in se* to name the dilemma Paul describes. The phrase means that our hearts often "turn in on themselves." Luther understood well that we all have this tendency to turn inward, living for ourselves rather than for others. In Luther's thinking, we are stuck in a cycle of our own making, never quite able to get out from underneath the shadow of our sinful selves. I think Luther is onto something here, but this fundamental distrust of human nature has sometimes meant that we Lutherans make little room for our own growth and development. Sally's story suggests a more nuanced version. Her story suggests that there is a path toward growth, but that paradoxically that path comes through our practices of care and concern for others. I have to admit that it's a little ironic that Sally experienced this most clearly not through her work at the church, but through her work at the utility company.

Opportunities

In mid-August of 2016, I received an email that changed the entire course of my career. The week before, I had run into a colleague at a conference. As we caught up, she mentioned that there was a position opening up at her institution, that she thought I would be perfect for it, but that she wanted to check with her dean first. When I opened the email that day, it read:

"Are you available on Friday at 3:00 pm your time? The dean would like to call you then about an opportunity that we have here."

I replied that I was available and that I was looking forward to the conversation. But honestly, I didn't think too much about it. When the dean and I did speak, he explained that the seminary was creating a new position, one that would need a particular set of talents. He thought I had that set of talents and he hoped that I would apply. Unlike many academic positions, however, this one was on the fast track. They wanted someone to begin as soon as possible, but no later than October.

October! I thought to myself, *That's not going to happen. I'm getting married in October.*

Even though the position sounded interesting, the timing was terrible. My fiancée (now wife) and I were in the middle of packing up our apartment. We were set to move in just two weeks, and I was about to leave for a ten-day study seminar in Greece. When I returned, I was supposed to begin my dissertation research. Between moving, the research work, and finalizing plans for the wedding, I wasn't sure how I could even consider the opportunity.

After many conversations, I threw my name in the hat for the position.

The next few months, though, were a whirlwind. By the time I received an offer, we had moved into our new apartment. Knowing there was a possibility I might get the job, we didn't unpack everything. We got married, went on our honeymoon, and returned to say goodbye to our friends in Boston—the place we had met and the place we had called home for four years.

We then loaded all our belongings into a large moving truck and packed our Jeep as full as humanly possible before driving to see family for Thanksgiving. The week after that, we unloaded everything in our new apartment in Iowa and I began my new job.

It was an exciting way to begin our marriage, to say the least. For me personally, it was a bit surreal. Six years earlier I had decided to pursue graduate studies with the hopes of becoming a seminary professor, but I had no idea if it would really happen.

My grades in seminary were good, but my college transcript revealed a Grade Point Average of barely a B. *Would I even get into a doctoral program?* Even if I did get in, would I cut it? Would I pass the famously difficult exams, and if I did, would I have the discipline necessary to complete a dissertation? My grandfather had started a doctoral program, but never finished. He used to remind me of that often. I think he regretted not finishing.

And yet here I was, not yet finished with my graduate studies, but starting a faculty position, nonetheless. I was genuinely surprised that someone was giving me the opportunity.

***

Leslie, the human resources executive, also began her career under some surprising circumstances. Perhaps that is part of what made her such an effective recruiter and manager. She knew the power of an opportunity firsthand. She especially understood what an opportunity could mean for someone who may or may not have deserved it. In one of my interviews with Leslie, I asked her about the distribution company at which she worked. I was especially interested in what caused her to stay at the same company for her entire career.

Here's what she said:

> We have a lot of jobs that are not glamorous, but it's a great place to work. We pay well. We pay bonuses. We have company events. We talk to our employees. We listen to our employees.

When I asked her to tell me about a time when she found her work particularly satisfying, she said:

> I think what's most satisfying, as I look back, is seeing people that were given an opportunity to work for a great company

and now seeing them today as the future leaders of the company. We gave them a job maybe when they were in college, and now they're supporting families. Or, when they started, they just wanted to work part time in a warehouse, and now they're running the warehouse. I mean, the director of warehousing that I work a lot with, we hired when he was sixteen. And I'm really proud of those stories. That's very satisfying.

I was surprised how often participants in my research named "opportunities"—and especially opportunities to grow—among those things which made their work meaningful. After all, an opportunity is really just a set of circumstances; it's really just a chance. As it turns out, a lot of people simply want to be given a chance.

Some of my participants made good money. A few made really good money. And while their financial success was certainly a part of the story they told, not one of them said their compensation or benefits were what made their work meaningful. Instead, they mentioned the quality of the work (Ben), the relationships they had through work (Sally), and the opportunities they were given or that they gave to others (Sally and Leslie). That stood out to me because that's what mattered to me too. I thought being a professional theologian was weird—and it is—but in most ways that job is like many others.

***

If you had read as many "theologies of work" as I have, you too would notice that there is little to no talk about opportunities. I believe that part of the reason for this is that these theologies have their origins in the medieval age, a time when there weren't many opportunities for social mobility. An opportunity at work doesn't mean that much when there's nothing at stake, when it is nearly impossible to improve your social standing or provide your children with a better future. Another reason for this lack of talk about opportunities is that more recent theologies of work have focused on how work changed after the Industrial Revolution. Those theologians are (rightly) concerned about things like massive unemployment, social inequality, and the dignity of workers. In short, these theologies approach work from a bird's-eye view.

My approach to thinking theologically about work is different. It is not necessarily better, but it is focused more on individual experiences, on the stories particular people tell about particular kinds of work. Only when you listen to ordinary workers do you hear things like, "Oh, what I found most meaningful is the opportunities I had."

I don't know if these workers realized it or not, but the presence of opportunities (or not) is actually an extraordinary theological idea. Jürgen Moltmann, one of the most influential theologians of the twentieth century, alludes to this in his book *A Theology of Hope*.[2] In a section that is really about sin, Moltmann writes that often when we talk about sin, we talk about trying to be God. Sometimes theologians call this sin in its "original form"—a reference to the way the serpent tempted Adam and Eve by saying that they too could be like God. But there is another side of sin, says Moltmann, and that's hopelessness and resignation.

Moltmann describes sin this way because, for him, faith or belief is grounded in hope—a hope in God's future. Belief requires hope, unbelief is a hopeless place with no future. Drawing on the words of another theologian, Moltmann reminds us that "it is not so much sin that plunges us into disaster, as rather despair."[3]

No matter where we encounter it, an *opportunity* is a path that leads away from hopelessness and despair. It represents a chance

---

2 Jürgen Moltmann, *Theology of Hope: On the Ground and the Implications of a Christian Eschatology* (Minneapolis: Fortress, 1993).

3 Moltmann, *Theology of Hope*, 23.

for something new. And it allows us to believe that things don't have to continue to be the way they currently are.

Admittedly, these opportunities at work may not have much to do with Christian hope or God's future. But I am increasingly convinced that our theologies must reflect the way life really is, and if that is true, then the raw materials of theology might look like experiences of hope in the face of despair wherever they show up.

***

Two years after I was given my first opportunity as a seminary professor, I was stuck. I was no longer growing or challenged in my role, and it was increasingly clear that there would be no future opportunities coming my way. The problem, though, was that I was so busy with work that I had little time for my dissertation research—the very thing that might well have been my ticket out of there. It got to the point that I could not even see or imagine a way out, and that's when I started to slip into a very dark place. At first I didn't recognize it, but through conversation with few trusted friends, I realized that I was depressed, and that I needed help.

I was still stuck in April of 2019 when I got another important email, this time from someone I didn't know. The sender was a faculty member at a seminary on the East Coast. The seminary had just received a large grant to conduct a national research study, and the person emailing me wanted to know whether I would be interested in applying for the position. This seminary also needed someone who could start as soon as possible.

This time, the timing could not have been better. Being offered that job was the beginning of the end for that cycle of despair. Thank God! After that experience, I doubt I could ever underestimate the power of an opportunity again.

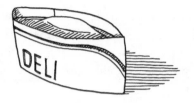

Mentors

I dedicated this book to my parents because the more I listened to the stories my participants were sharing, the more they reminded me that my three brothers and I have been my parents' life's work. My parents, perhaps like all good parents, thought we boys could do anything, that the sky was the limit.

Of course they thought the world of us! That's what parents do!

Because of my father's work, we moved often as a family. By the time I was starting high school, I had already lived in three different states. Each time we moved, we found a new Lutheran church to attend. It was at church that I met Marc and Dana Reed—two additional adult role models who played a significant role during my high school years.

I spent quite a bit of time at the Reeds' house. Sometimes I would just show up unannounced and walk right in. When I met them, they already had three biological children. They would go on to adopt two more. In some ways, they had already adopted me. At one point, a framed picture of my prom date and I sat on their mantle with their other family photos.

Marc and Dana were mentors to me during those turbulent adolescent years. They listened to me through breakups with girl-friends and through the agonies of college decisions. No matter what, I knew they would be supportive voices beyond my parents. Just as important, they recognized gifts in me that I could not always see myself.

***

Today, John oversees the meat departments at over one hundred locations of the grocery store for which he started working during his high school years. He has come a long way since then, but not without the help of mentors along the way. As he put it:

> *The CEO of the company was a huge mentor in my life. He took the time even though he was running a corporation. You could walk up to the guy, and if you had a question for him, he would stop whatever he was doing and then help you through that stuff. So that was really special.*

That mentoring relationship with the CEO had a significant impact on John. So much so that when I asked John about a time that he found his work particularly satisfying, this is what he told me:

> *What matters most to me and my life is taking somebody . . . and spending an extra two or three minutes with them. I've mentored quite a few people through their divorces. I've tried to help them identify or see the triggers that were in my [own] life, that led to my [own] divorce. [Like] putting too much focus on trying to be a super-achiever rather than being involved with your family. I had a huge imbalance there. You can see that in people's lives pretty quickly when you're involved with them on a personal level. When I come into a store, I just observe their body language. I can usually tell whether or not somebody's having a good day. I try to spend more time on trying to find out what's going on with them and show genuine interest in that too. It's not just about what's going on behind the meat counter.*

Much of how we typically think about economic activity, including work, is grounded in the notion of *self-interest*. Adam

Smith, who is sometimes called the "father of modern economics," theorized that the interests of all could usually be accomplished when individuals each act in their own self-interest. In fact, according to Smith, all we need to be concerned about is ourselves.[4]

It's difficult to see John's efforts to create a mentoring environment in his workplace as an act of self-interest. Cynically, perhaps, we could say that John is taking a few extra minutes of his time to show interest in his managers because he thinks that if they feel valued and appreciated, they are more likely to go the extra mile for the company. Worker morale and productivity are closely connected, and ultimately John's self-interest is to maximize productivity and profits. John's efforts only *appear* benevolent.

That is a possible interpretation. But more likely, John really does care about the personal well-being those who work under him. Self-interest drove him to become a workaholic earlier in his career, and while that may have earned him a promotion or two, he realizes it also cost him his marriage. Managers who have a poor work-life balance may actually make John's corporate reports look better, but John concluded long ago that it's not worth the cost.

***

Mentoring, at least from a Christian perspective, has the potential to cultivate transformative relationships. Author and researcher Sharon Daloz Parks has written about the significant role that mentors can play in helping young adults find their feet in today's complex world. Parks' research focuses on young adults, but she is quick to point out that her insights apply more broadly because at each stage of life, we need others who have gone before us to show us the way.

---

4 Miroslav Volf, *Work in the Spirit: Toward a Theology of Work* (1991; repr., Eugene, OR: Wipf and Stock, 2001), 53.

The term *mentor* is easily misused. Perhaps because it can be so difficult today to find authentic meaningful relationships of care, popular discourse often invokes the term "mentor" when other descriptions might be more appropriate. Parks insists that the term mentor is best reserved for "a distinct role in the story of human becoming."[5] Listening to stories from John and others about the role that mentoring has played in their working lives, I am inclined to agree that mentoring is more than mere supervision, advising, or even friendship.

Mentors offer recognition. It sounds rather basic, but we all have a need to be "seen," to be recognized for who we are and what we have to offer. John knows that the CEO recognizing him early on at the grocery store set him on the management path. Now he's in a position to recognize others.

Mentors offer support. Support in this sense is more than just being a listening ear; it is about championing the potential of others in ways they cannot do for themselves. John spent much of his early life struggling in school and comparing himself to his high-achieving brother. It took a mentor to point out that his people skills could take him places no one expected.

Mentors offer conversation. Conversations marked by mutual respect and openness can be hard to come by. Those conversations with the CEO helped John find his way and find his voice. Some mentors, like John, are aware and intentional about their role. Others, however, may not always realize the mentoring moments they have extended to others.

Mentors offer tough love and ask tough questions. Often mentors do hold some kind of formal authority over others. But what allows them to challenge others through tough love and ask the big questions is their willingness to set aside their own agenda and power plays out of genuine care. John knows his fancy title

---

5 Sharon Daloz Parks, *Big Questions, Worthy Dreams: Mentoring Young Adults in Their Search for Meaning, Purpose, and Faith* (San Francisco: Jossey-Bass, 2000), 128.

can be intimidating, so it takes an extra effort on his part to get to know his colleague beyond who they are at work.

Even if it is clear that mentors play a significant role for those coming up behind them, it is less clear what is explicitly theological about this. *How are mentoring relationships connected to God's work in the world?* Parks writes that all good mentors know "learning that matters is ultimately a spiritual, transforming activity, intimately linked with the whole of life."[6] I agree that the process of our becoming who we are has a spiritual dimension to it. It has a degree of transcendence baked into it. But I think John's story also suggests that mentoring can be a kind of Christian practice—a Christian way of exercising power and authority. Mentoring can be an alternative kind of authority. Not the kind of authority that gets its way by exerting itself or by issuing edicts and demands. Rather, mentors begin their work by setting aside their own interests and agendas to listen. In a world driven by self-interest, mentoring is about others' interests. In a world in which power is often accumulated and protected at all costs, mentoring levels the field.

Which is not to say that mentoring is one-sided self-sacrifice. Often mentors like John find that they learn and grow just as much as the person being mentored. That's exactly why John finds so much meaning in the mentoring he does.

***

I suspect that because of Marc and Dana, I have always sought out the help and guidance of mentors. In high school, they were not my only mentors. Besides them, I remember Brian and Vicki, my two youth directors, and Anton, my pastor. In college, it was Greg, the campus pastor, and Terry, Jill, Donna, and Jerry, the owners of the coffee shop. I think also of Aaron, a singer-songwriter for

---

6 Parks, *Big Questions, Worthy Dreams*, 128.

whom I worked one summer. During my years in seminary, I recall Patricia, Chris, Eileen, and Mary Sue. In Boston, my two doctoral advisors, Mary Elizabeth and Nancy, went far beyond the call of duty, and a pastor named Tim was definitely more of a mentor than a boss. Nate and Thomas both mentored me in that first faculty position, though they probably don't know it.

I am not sure what it says about me that I needed twenty mentors, but I definitely needed each of them.

"We're Not Going to Fire You"

Years ago, I was working part time at a congregation when I learned that I had been accepted into a doctoral program. I shared the news with the pastor and the rest of the congregation, though it would be several months before leaving my position. I immediately got to work on a transition plan. Much of my work at the church had been building a team and working with other lay leaders in the congregation. As I thought about the weeks and months ahead, I began to imagine what it would look like to wind down my day-to-day involvement gradually and hand over key tasks to others. The congregation had come a long way during the previous three years, and I was excited to see them step up to the challenge my transition would bring.

A few weeks later, I got a call from the pastor inviting me to lunch with the president of the congregation. This was not all that unusual, so I put it in my calendar. When I arrived at the restaurant a few days later, I instantly knew something was amiss. Joe, the president of the congregation, had a look on his face. He looked uncomfortable. *I wonder if something is going on at work, or maybe even at home.*

Shortly after our food arrived and after some more small talk, I figured out what that look on Joe's face was all about.

"Tim, we really appreciate all that you've done at the congregation," the pastor said. "But we can tell you're on your way out. There are so many things we've talked about doing and you're not doing any of that. We think you should end your time at the church this coming Sunday."

Wait what? I thought to myself. *Am I getting fired?*

Not knowing how to respond, I told the pastor that I needed a little time to think about it, but that I would give him my answer the next day. The rest of the lunch was awkward. Now I understood what that look on Joe's face was all about. The pastor moved on to sports talk and I pushed my food around my plate until it was time to go.

Later that afternoon, I worried about what I would do. It was months before I would be moving across the country for graduate school, and in the meantime, I had rent and other bills to pay. Plus, I still did not know how I was even going to pay for that move. I also worried about how my loss of income would affect my housemate—a friend who was a part-time pastor who needed a housemate that could pay his portion of the rent.

To be honest, I did not understand what was happening, much less why. I needed to figure out what I would tell the pastor the next day. Time was running out.

***

Of all the workers I interviewed, James had the clearest sense of a calling. He understood that his work as a government employee was a form of public service. He was working to improve the lives of everyone who lived in his city. He used the language of the vocational script, and he was confident that God was involved in his working life. When I asked him whether his faith ever came up at work, this is what he told me:

> *The last two years, a colleague's health been going down-hill, and it was very visible that he was losing his battle with cancer. He kept saying, "Well, you guys are just going to let me go. You're going to fire me." I said, "Mark, we're not going to do that. You're a valuable member of this community and this workplace. And I value your work." I think that was my faith—letting him know that he has people here who support him. God is present. That's helped me. I do that in a lot of my interactions with the staff. You've got to be careful because I'm a government employee, but I can get a feel for when I can bring up the G-word. You know and talk about faith and try to bring that in.*
>
> *The guy that sits in the next cubicle over, he's in property management and a member at my church. The gal that used to sit on the other side of me, she was the treasurer. She came to our church because a colleague and I invited her. So you just don't know but you extend that invitation. Our pastor is drilling this into the congregation. You never know what might happen. I mean, that's an instance where I try to be reasonable and listen, and hopefully my faith is coming across to everybody. Even though I might say a few G-words once in a while just because they understand that my heart's in the right spot.*

James and several others in the study had concrete stories just like this one. Stories about times in which, by their account, their Christian faith inspired them to act with care and concern for their fellow colleagues. Of course, it is not only Christians who extend such care at work, but for those in this study, their faith was what animated their empathy and kind actions. They saw moments like the one above as examples of how Christians might put their faith into action in the workplace.

***

Researchers have long been interested in better understanding the role of religion in the United States. Social scientists have often approached this task by measuring the beliefs and practices of churchgoers and non-churchgoers alike. One special concern for these researchers is the *strength* of belief and commitment; determining this helps them understand which groups are more or less religious.

The problem is: *What exactly is normal when it comes to being religious?*

For example, what about someone who believes most of the things we have come to expect Christians to believe, but perhaps they are not so sure about everything that is in the Bible and, perhaps, they are not sure that Christianity is the only way to know God. They sometimes attend church, but they also take time on the weekends to enjoy the outdoors. Is this person less religious than someone who checks all the right boxes and attends every Sunday?

A few decades ago, many researchers would have said that such a person is not all that religious. They might have used more technical terms, but they thought of such people as lukewarm churchgoers. Sociologist Nancy Ammerman changed the conversation, however, when she pointed out that among mainline Protestants, the kind of Christian I described above is actually really common, and that they should really be understood on their own terms rather than comparing them to the standards of Evangelical Protestants, who tend to focus more on checking the correct belief boxes. These Christians, Ammerman suggested, held a "Golden Rule" ethic—meaning that their faith was more grounded in doing good in the world and in practices of care than traditional beliefs. These Golden Rule Christians are not necessarily less religious: they are differently religious.[7]

James' story includes two different practices of faith. The first is exactly this kind of Golden Rule practice that Ammerman signals. James extends care and support to his colleague with cancer because, for him, it is the right thing to do. The second is his invitation to others at work to join his church, a practice his pastor regularly encourages.

I wonder whether God views these two practices equally. I am not suggesting that inviting people to church is a bad thing; it is often a very good thing. But an invitation to church and a faith-based intervention that offers genuine empathy and saves a cancer patient's employment do not seem even close to being the same. The thing is, in all my years attending church, I, too, have regularly been encouraged to invite others to church. But I do not recall many sermons that encouraged basic acts of human decency. From the stories I heard from these workers, there does not appear to be a shortage of information about where to go to church. However, there does seem to be a shortage of basic human decency. I think James is right: our Christian faith calls us to intervene with care and support; it calls us to show up to those around us who are suffering and say, "Hey, you know what? I'm here, God is here. Let's figure this out." I could be wrong, but that seems more Christian than an invitation to church.

***

Back to my dilemma at the restaurant. Not knowing what else to do, I reached out to a former professor and mentor. We talked it out and he said that it sounded as if the pastor and I had very different ideas about what a good ending looked like. The pastor

---

7   Nancy Tatom Ammerman, "Golden Rule Christianity: Lived Religion in the American Mainstream," in *Lived Religion in America: Toward a History of Practice*, ed. David Hall (Princeton: Princeton University Press, 1997), 196.

wanted to wind things up—in a triumphant full sprint to the finish line. I, on the other hand, wanted to wind it down step by step until I was not really needed.

He was right. But I still had to figure out what to do the next day. That night, I called Joe, the congregation president, and we had a long talk. I explained what I thought was going on and I explained that I could not afford to quit the job early. Joe shared with me that the idea of my early departure was the pastor's preference, but he did not think other leaders were in on it. He also assured me that no matter what I decided, I had his support. He felt horrible about the situation I was in.

That meant the world to me and knowing that gave me the courage I needed. The next day, I called the pastor and I told him I thought leaving that Sunday was a bad idea. Many in the congregation would be blind-sided and a sudden departure would sever all the relationships I had built there. Plus, I could not afford it, so if that is what he wanted, he would have to fire me.

We split the difference. I still left earlier than I had anticipated and earlier than I could afford, but I had the chance to say some proper goodbyes. Looking back now, I am especially grateful for Joe's basic human decency.

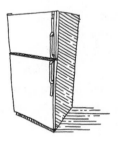

"Farmers Feed the World"

If disclosing your profession is one occupational hazard of being a theologian, another is going to church. Of course, the church has played a significant role in my life, and today I spend the majority of my week studying and teaching about things we do at church. But it is hard to spend that much time on something like the church and not have strong feelings about the way it should and should not be. And that is the occupational hazard. It can be difficult simply to sit there and be fed.

**

When I met Sam, a farmer and small-business owner, he told me that his wife sometimes asks when he will retire. "What would I do in retirement? I like to run a farm and play cards once in a while in the morning. And I like to visit with the guys. I like to fish. I like to golf. But if I could do that all the time, I wouldn't like it at all."

It makes sense to me that Sam would feel that way. Of all those I interviewed for this project, Sam had one of the most romantic stories about meaning of his work. When I asked him whether he ever thought about his work as a calling, he said:

> *I think we feed the world. I've said that for years. We feed the world.*
>
> *We may not be in charge of getting it where it belongs, but we're in a country where we are the granary for the rest of the world. We just are. We take a lot of pride in our crops. I've been a no-tiller for thirty-some years; I don't till the ground. Most people thought I was nuts from the start, but soil conservation is very important for the ground that feeds the world.*

Because I set out to listen to these stories with the assumption that God was already at work in the lives of these workers, I promised myself that I would try to hear and understand each worker on their own terms. That meant, among other things, that

I would not challenge or reframe their understandings. Whenever possible, I would use their own words and frames of meaning. Only after listening to them would I attempt to reflect theologically on what was most at stake in their stories and what those aspects meant to them.

I have to admit, however, that Sam's initial story about farmers feeding the world sounded suspect to me. For one thing, farming was just one thing Sam did. At the time, he was helping his forty-year-old son get into farming. That is significant because our nation's farmers are getting older and older. In prior generations, farms were passed down through the family. These days, the children of farmers often want nothing to do with farming, and that is disrupting this traditional way of work and life. But farming was just a small part of what Sam does. He runs two businesses and employs nine people. He also volunteers twice a week as an announcer for the basketball games of local schools. They actually put him in their sports hall of fame for his dedication to the sport.

So at best, farming seemed like only part of Sam's story.

Then there was that phrase itself: *farmers feed the world*. It sounded too much like the kind of thing you would see on a bumper sticker. And sure enough, it took me less than ten minutes on the internet before I found a bumper sticker with those exact words. *Of course, I bought one.*

I understood what Sam was saying, but he was the third farmer to whom I had talked, and the others had given me a tutorial on local agricultural crops. The reality is that Sam grew field corn and soybeans just like the others. Field corn can be used to feed livestock, but it's not the kind of corn you and I eat. In fact, most of the corn grown in the state where Sam lives becomes ethanol. While corn is more renewable than petroleum, adding it to our gasoline to run our cars still creates significant air pollution; it actually reduces fuel efficiency, and it tends to affect the price of corn and fuel for consumers negatively. And those soybeans? Well, most of them end up in China, which is a very big country, but it is not exactly "the world." I am pretty sure I read somewhere in the Bible that man cannot live by soybeans alone.

Personally, I was skeptical, but I had made that promise about listening, and I intended to keep it. But then I heard this story on public radio about a children's book being published by the North Dakota Farmers Union. The president of the union was being interviewed and he summarized the book this way:

> *Well, the story talks about how everyone works on the family farm, and it kind of runs you through . . . a part of a day, a little bit of a harvest, Grandma out in the garden gathering vegetables. And the combine actually breaks down. And they find a way to get that combine fixed with the help of Grandpa, who knows everything. And then it kind of shows how that grain gets to the market and gets to the world. So the family farm feeds the world.*[8]

Wait: "Farmers feed the world" is something Sam has said for years, *and* it's the text of a bumper sticker, *and* it's the punch line of a children's book? I wanted to take Sam seriously, but it was starting to feel as if one of the stories he tells himself and others about the meaning of his work is actually propaganda!

Propaganda, in my humble opinion, does not make good source material for theology.

As I set out to write about Sam's story for the first time, I had highlighted some of the key passages from his interviews; he was quite the character, and he had some great stories to tell. I returned to those transcripts in search of the fuller picture. Maybe I had not understood Sam as well as I thought I had. Maybe I had

---

8 National Public Radio, "Children's Book, 'Our Family Farm,' Sells Thousands of Copies," hosted by Lulu Garcia-Navarro, Weekend Edition Sunday, on NPR, October 13, 2019, https://www.npr.org/2019/10/13/769848605/childrens-book-our-family-farm-sells-thousands-of-copies.

missed something else he had said, or perhaps I had overlooked an important link between Sam's various projects. That is when I rediscovered this side comment Sam made, almost a throwaway line in the middle of a rambling response that had, frankly, gotten a little off track from my line of questioning. He was rehearsing how a typical week goes. As he put it:

> *Mostly, I get up in the morning and go to the truck shop, where I have eight employees—but I operate a little different than most places. Everyone is given a truck that they take care of, and they operate, and they're paid on a percentage. If they're doing repair work, they get paid by the hour doing that. My job is to make sure that there's work for them to do, and their job is to figure how they're going to get it done.*
>
> *Normally, every afternoon, about 4:30 or 5:00, we have this table out in the shop with a refrigerator close by. We sit and visit about everything. On Sunday morning, one of my employees that's been with me probably thirty years now, that's his life. He'll go down there just to see what's going on. A lot of times, if I come down on Sunday morning, I'll find that they got their own church service going on. It really ain't a church service, but the table will be full of friends. They'll talk for an hour or two, and then they break up. It's their community.*

That last line—"It's their community"—stood out to me. When I reread it, I remembered that Sam had also told me that when the town's bowling alley was in jeopardy of closing, he bought it just to keep it open. He felt it was an important place for the youth in the community.

I also remembered Sam's response when federal authorities cracked down on undocumented migrant workers in the town's meatpacking plant. He was one of the first volunteers to show up at the Catholic church that the migrant workers attended. They organized food, shelter, and other necessities for those who suddenly had their families ripped apart. That confirmed my sense that when Sam talked about "community," he was not just talking about afternoon shop talk. His sense of community was about practicing care for others—both for his longtime employees and for relative strangers alike.

Sam may not literally feed the world, but he certainly has a track record of setting the table and providing for his community. He grows field corn, soybeans, and a sense of belonging for those in his local community. I am not sure this is what he meant by those four words—*farmers feed the world*. But it does reflect Sam's broader sense of meaning and purpose.

***

Sometimes I wish there were a simpler version of church where people could just sit down together over a meal, tell stories, and talk about things that actually mattered to them.

Maybe I could stop by Sam's shop next Sunday morning. Sam said there is room at the table and that the refrigerator is well-stocked.

"We're All in This Together"

Working at a restaurant is a team sport. When I worked at the restaurant, each shift would begin with brief meeting in the bar area. Everyone would be gathered around: servers, bussers, line cooks, and hosts. One of the managers would usually remind us of the day's special and update us on anything else we needed to know before the shift began: *"Today's special is the pork chop, and whoever sells the most pork chops gets dinner on me. We've only got one host tonight, so be nice to Becky. Give her some space to do her job. I don't want to see any servers at the host stand, you got me? Okay, everyone, have a great service."*

Or something like that. Afterward, everyone would head to their respective places in the restaurant, the doors would be opened, and soon the first guests would walk in. If everyone did their job, the service would go well. If not, everyone was in for a long night. That is just the way it goes. Everyone needs each other during dinner service; the moment you do not have each other's backs, the whole ship starts to sink.

***

Valerie reminded me of all those dinner shifts at the restaurant when she shared with me a few times she found her work particularly satisfying:

> *Probably the best four years of my teaching experience were when I taught at a post-secondary technical school. It's very similar to the community college system. The first four years I taught there, I was teaching adults. Those people wanted to be there. Not all of my students were great students, but they're paying money, so they usually wanted to be there. They were engaged. They wanted to learn what you had to share with them. I really loved those four years of teaching. That was an interesting experience. I taught in a very large school district, but it was a very poor school district. It was the staff that really, really had to work together in order to be successful. As the computer teacher, I would save all of my*

paper that had been thrown in the recycle bin and would go through it and flip it over, stack it, and then take it across the hall to the Art Department because they didn't have any paper. So you really learned how to help each other. And I really valued that experience and learned a lot; I didn't understand that experience until I left.

Then I came here, which at the time was a very, very affluent school district with a completely different attitude. It was almost shocking to me to see how territorial teachers were instead of "We're all in this together."

Like other teachers, Valerie found her work meaningful when she could see the growth and development of her students. That was clear from her description of that first teaching job. But unlike other teachers, Valerie discovered the hard way that being a good teacher was not just about the students. It couldn't be, because teaching is also a team sport. Everyone needs each other for everything to work. That's how Valerie saw it.

***

By the time Valerie shared this story with me, I had begun to use the phrase "daily grind" as shorthand for many of the experiences these workers were sharing. *Daily grind* was shorthand for the struggle to meet the demands of one's work. It was shorthand for the way work takes its toll. And it was shorthand for the day-in, day-out persistence of all this. What surprised me was that this daily grind was present in stories that cut across socioeconomic levels. It didn't seem to matter whether one was a pharmacist, a banker, a teacher, or a hairdresser. Work was a daily grind.

This story was a further revelation about the daily grind of work. When the daily grind is a shared experience, and when that shared experience fosters a special sense of trust and a shared sense of mutual belonging among workers, solidarity becomes a powerful counter-narrative to work's most dehumanizing effects. Without solidarity, the daily grind just wears one down. With solidarity, workers like Valerie can find a sense of meaning and purpose that transcends the work itself.

In my search for new ways of thinking about the relationship between our working lives and theology, I discovered that for about a decade in the mid-twentieth century, French priests tried to close a gap between the working poor and the Catholic Church by joining them at work. At the time, the working poor had become especially disillusioned with the church and its teachings. Many were turning to atheism.

These priests knew that these workers—many of them factory workers or laborers who worked on the docks—were unlikely to come to them; they were going to have to stand shoulder-to-shoulder with these workers and preach less with their words and more with their actions. It's revealing that these priests also knew traditional seminary education would not prepare them for the ministry they imagined. So they created new kinds of schools where those preparing for the priesthood would still hear lectures on theology, but they would also read Karl Marx and discuss current events over breakfast.

At first it was awkward. Some employers were understandably hesitant to hire priests. Explaining why they weren't married was, well, also a bit uncomfortable; it was shocking for some to learn they had been working alongside a priest for weeks. Eventually, though, the priests were accepted. As one worker-priest put it:

> We had experienced the factory atmosphere, the continual persecution, the lack of liberty, initiative and confidence, the scornful and condescending smiles of the foremen, the hush-money of the management, the penalties, the arbitrary firings, the lay-offs. We have experienced everything that hides behind the language of production needs; the

sending away of those who are no longer young enough or
lively enough and for others, infernal work, the cadence,
the incessant march against the clock, the physical and
nerve-wracking exhaustion, the nightmares while sleep-
ing and the habitual deception on payday of ridiculously
low wages.[9]

Like Valerie, the worker-priests experienced solidarity within
the daily grind of factory work and found meaning in being in
it together.

Almost as soon as the worker-priest experiment began, it was
deemed suspect. It only took a few years before two of these priests
were summoned to Rome for questioning. In 1952, less than a
decade after it began, two worker-priests were arrested during a
political demonstration. While in custody, they were beaten and
interrogated as "communists." The press rushed to their defense,
and soon a full-blown scandal erupted.

This set into motion a series of events: First, the bishops
insisted on a more traditional form of priestly ministry. Then
the new seminaries were closed. By 1954, the Vatican ended
the experiment. But solidarity is a powerful—even transformative—reality. After many discussions among themselves and
with their bishops, nearly two-thirds of the worker-priests continued working in the factories and on the docks, no matter
the cost.

During the experiment, no other theologian had a greater
influence on the worker-priests than Marie-Dominique Chenu, a
Dominican theologian hardly known outside of Catholic circles.
Chenu led the worker-priests in retreats during which he invited
them to reflect theologically on what they were experiencing
among the working poor.

---

9 Oscar L. Arnal, *Priests in Working-Class Blue: The History of the Worker-
Priests (1943–1953)* (New York: Paulist Press, 1986), 81.

After the experiment had ended, Chenu was expelled from Paris. In exile, he wrote a book called *The Theology of Work: An Exploration*, in which he tried to put the experiences of those worker-priests front and center. He wrote:

> The tragic gulf between mechanization and humanity cannot be bridged by the usual conventional phrases on the dignity of manual labor having been restored by Christianity, on the value of work as an educative discipline, or even, at the doctrinal level, on its ascetic function in a world where suffering, sin, and liberation are linked together. The traditional images of potter, blacksmith, and peasant with which the Bible furnished the old theologians, are not only inadequate but often encouraged a resentment against the machine and led to debatable praise of craftworking, small-scale proprietorship, the patriarchal family and the peasantry, which is both bad theology and vain romanticism.[10]

Chenu goes on to conclude that the Industrial Revolution had brought on an entirely new set of issues that theologians needed to address. It might be the case, says Chenu, that modern economic and political systems have created new kinds of hardship and toil for the world of work, but ironically it has also enlivened a spirit of solidarity among workers. Chenu suggested that this spirit of solidarity offered new ways of understanding liberation and what he called "social maturity."[11] I bet Valerie would call it *really being in this thing together*.

I wonder what a contemporary worker-priest movement would look like today? What would happen if our pastors joined

---

10 Marie-Dominique Chenu, *The Theology of Work: An Exploration*, trans. Lilian Soiron (Chicago: Henry Regnery, 1966), 8.

11 Chenu, *Theology of Work*, 53.

the corporate world, took up farming in the Midwest, or rented a chair at the nearby salon? And what kind of theology would appear if every once in a while, these pastors took a retreat together to reflect on their concrete experiences of the daily grind?

Would it last? Probably not. Would their higher-ups shut it down? Probably.

***

There is a certain kind of solidarity in higher education. At conferences we get together in the evenings over dinner and commiserate. We complain to one another about this or that and it feels good to laugh (or cry) about it with others. Occasionally, we theologians collaborate on a book project or on organizing a conference. But, most days, I begin my work by slipping into my private office early in the morning. I usually get there before everyone else. I do my best work in the morning, so I start with whatever requires my most focused attention. If I am lucky, no one will bother me for several hours before I have to turn to emails and attend meetings or appointments. In fact, the fewer meetings and appointments I have with other people the better.

No, it's definitely not a team sport.

What Matters in the End

When I began this project, I had a suspicion that the age of my participants would be important. A few years before, I had done a similar project with a group of thirty-year-olds. They, too, had interesting working lives, but their stories were just beginning. In a way, that made questions of meaning and purpose more elusive. They had ideas, of course, about what their working lives might mean, but it was hard for them to say for sure. That's why I wanted to interview workers who were close to retiring, or at least were of retirement age. I was interested in their *retrospective* understandings of work.

As a researcher, I had been taught how to interview others. Bruce, the professor who taught us, was a former student of Noam Chomsky, the famous linguist who believed that language was a uniquely human capacity. I thought that was ironic because Bruce said it was important to practice asking questions, and he used to practice on his dog.

I didn't have a dog, so I would practice reciting my questions out loud in the car on my way to interviews. This worked fine, for the most part. Eventually, I settled in and found my rhythm in these interviews. I began to get a sense for how some questions were easier and more effective to ask later on in the interview, after I had demonstrated that I was willing to just listen.

I say this worked fine for the most part, but there was one question that never got easier. The question itself wasn't hard, but it was deeply existential in a way that was different from the rest of my questions. At the end of each interview, I would say something like this: *"Thanks again for taking the time to share your story with me. There's just one more question I have. Given all that you have shared today about your work and your faith, how would you like to be remembered in the end?"*

The question was usually followed by a bit of silence. It was never more than a few seconds, but it could feel much longer. It got harder and harder to ask this question because over time the responses had a profound impact on me. I am not sure what I thought people would say, but I found myself deeply moved by the simplicity of what actually matters in the end of our very complicated lives. Here is a sample of their responses:

- *That I cared and that I loved them.*
- *I actually, I just want to be remembered as somebody who helped, not who judged, but who helped.*
- *She was a follower of Christ.*

- *I would hope people would remember me for being kind, a hard worker, but I think for being kind. Someone who tried to build faith. Build his own faith and build the faith of others around him while he was doing it. I think that's probably it.*
- *Well, I think when it comes right down to it, relationships— that I loved people, and I poured my life into people, and that I loved God and I tried to live out my life with God every day. I don't think there's anybody I know that doesn't know I'm a Christian. So I hope that the bottom line would be, 'She lived a life well that reflected who [she is] in Christ, whether it was at home or in church or at work.' It wasn't a perfect life, but it was a life well-lived, meaning that I tried.*
- *I would like to be remembered as an honest, caring, giving person.*
- *That I was honest. That I was true to my convictions. Maybe moderately successful, whatever that is. That I was committed to family, and faith, and what was important regardless of what was taking place.*
- *Oh. I guess just kind, generous, respectful.*
- *I would like to be remembered as a decent guy who tried to help people, who had a good sense of humor, and tried to make this world a better place.*
- *I guess I would say, I don't care that anyone actually remembers me. I used to think that that was important. I want my family to have that warm, fuzzy feeling when they think about me. And that Jesus and God were important in my life. As far as the rest of the world, I don't really care that they know who I was. Child of God, I guess.*

Within these, there is some theology—literally some "God-talk," but mostly what matters in the end is even more basic: the desire to be remembered as a good person. These responses to my final question reminded me that however one finds meaning and purpose in their work (or if they don't find that!), it is still just one part of a larger whole.

Some scholars of religion have suggested that modern life is compartmentalized; that each domain of our lives—work, family, church, etc.—plays by their own rules so that the values and habits that we find in one do not easily translate into the others. In this way our lives of faith have become largely private matters. Paying attention to what matters in the end, however, seems to call this idea into question. It may be the case that we learn to play a complex game in life where we are somewhat different people at work, at home, and at church. And it may even be the case that there are limits to bringing the world of work and the world of faith together. But all of that can still be woven together into a coherent whole through the stories we tell. In the end, we have a *life* story, not a work story or a faith story or a family story. It's just one story: ours.

One of the most common theological responses to modern work is a lament of capitalism's relentless emphasis on productivity. At work one hears there is never too much productivity and profits. The church's response is to emphasize sabbath rest. These theologians are also quick to point toward an American "Protestant work ethic," or in other words, the idea that capitalism required a wellspring of disciplined, hard-working laborers and that Protestant theology itself underwrote these values, giving economic action spiritual significance. Whether theology played a role in the development of capitalism is a matter of debate, but reflecting on their ultimate legacies, these workers rarely mentioned their professional success.

At other times the American Dream may be more discernible in the stories we tell about our working lives, but not so in the end. The responses above came from those who make six figures and those who make half that. They came from those who were quite satisfied with their career and those who were not. In fact, with every other question, there were significant differences among these workers. But on this question—*How do you want to be remembered in the end?*—they were remarkably of one mind.

It appears that what matters most has more to do with who we are than what we have accomplished.

And this brings us full circle, back to the vocational script and Martin Luther's writings on vocation. Remember that Luther actually wrote about vocation in two different ways. He wrote about a *general* sense of vocation, or in other words, the call to become a Christian, and a *particular* sense of vocation, or in other words, the call to a specific role. It is in the latter use of the term that we can talk about the call to be a teacher, a parent, or a citizen. The vocational script suggests that we can find our callings in these specific roles. It is interesting that when I asked these workers how they wanted to be remembered, their imaginations turned not to specific roles they had, but to a more general concern: a way of being. Collectively, their responses suggest that this way of being is a *Christian* way of being, but perhaps even more important than that is that they pointed to a way of being *human*—a way of being marked by things like kindness, honesty, faithfulness, generosity, and decency.

We theologians have spent a good deal of energy developing scripts to help others make sense of how God might be calling them in the future. So much of what we call vocational discernment has to do with what we might do next in our working lives. But it appears that there is a very different kind of vocational reflection at play when we engage in life-review, when we invite others to take stock of their lives. It is a way of doing theology by way of listening to stories of faith at work.

These *lived* vocations offer a glimpse of God's work in the world, but if we are going to learn from these lives, we may need new practices to hear them on their own terms. The chapter that follows is my attempt to outline at least one such practice: *testimony.*

6

Post-Script

Why We Need to Tell More Stories

Many people are looking for an ear that will listen. They do not find it among Christians, because these Christians are talking where they should be listening. But he who can no longer listen to his brother will soon be no longer listening to God either; he will be doing nothing but prattle in the presence of God too.

—Dietrich Bonhoeffer, *Life Together*

I set out on this project because I wanted to know what difference Christian faith made in the midst of everyday lives. In the end, I discovered that this question was more complicated than I imagined. Faith, or *lived* faith anyway, does not easily fit into prescribed storylines. Still, I heard many stories of faith at work.

If one asks, it is not all that difficult to find stories of Christians openly sharing their faith at work. Sometimes that looks like letting a colleague know that someone is praying for them. Other times it looks like inviting others to church. These kinds of stories are actually quite common.

One can also find stories where Christian faith itself is implicit, but no less at work. I heard over and over that Christian faith motivates a whole range of commitments and actions at work: kind interactions with colleagues, a commitment to stewarding the earth's resources, motivation for getting into a profession, and so on. As virtuous as these stories are, neither of these two kinds of stories were themselves what I was looking for.

What I really wanted to know is what kind of resource Christianity is for making sense of one's working life. I wanted to know, in their own words and on their own terms, how ordinary people of faith find meaning and purpose at work and whether that meaning and purpose has any relationship to their faith.

And *that* is a much more difficult to uncover because our work means so many different things, and those meanings are not easy to separate from the larger meaning of our lives.

The most universal patterns of meaning reflect what scholars have come to call "the human condition," or in other words, what it means to navigate a life with all of its possibilities and limits. Writing about this, Hannah Arendt, the Holocaust-survivor-turned-philosopher, observed that while we are all humans, and therefore share in this thing we call humanity, it is also the case that nobody is ever the same as anyone else who has ever lived, lives, or will live.[1] To talk about the meaning of *our* lives is to speak of things that are shared across vast oceans of human difference.

It is not only these individual differences that complicate matters; work itself is extraordinarily varied. Here I do not only have paid work in mind. Farming is not very similar to teaching and teaching is not very similar to running a trucking company or volunteering in the community or parenting. All of these are work.

We can think of each kind of work as having its own game and its own "rules of the game," or put differently, they each have their own sets of values, habits, and goals. Most of us learn how to play a number of "games" across the arenas of our everyday lives. We learn to play one game at work and another one at home, church, and so on. But the diversity of people and their work

---

1 Michael Jackson, *The Politics of Storytelling: Variations on a Theme by Hannah Arendt* (Copenhagen: Museum Musculanum Press/University of Copenhagen, 2013), 15.

seems to resist a one-size-fits-all approach for reflecting theologically on our working lives. If the vocational script is the only one in our repertoire, I doubt we theologians and pastors will be able to meet others where they really are.

So how can we begin to develop new ways of thinking theologically about our everyday lives? The truth is, I'm still working at figuring it out.

For quite some time, theology has done its work from a rather privileged position. For centuries, ordinary people of faith looked to their religious leaders for the answers, and their leaders sometimes obliged with ready-made answers to all of life's most important questions. But that is no longer the game theologians must play. Some of my colleagues (including some whom I deeply admire) may be happy playing that old game on an ever-shrinking field with fewer and fewer interested in our work. Personally, I find that possibility dissatisfying.

I do, however, suspect that if we are to discover new ways of thinking theologically about our everyday lives, we may have to admit that Dietrich Bonhoeffer was right. In his spiritual classic, *Life Together*, Bonhoeffer made a poignant observation that seems as true today as it was in the 1930s when he penned it.[2] We Christians seem to spend more time talking than listening. Bonhoeffer especially singled out pastors as culprits of this, but I can assure you that we theologians belong in their company as well. Bonhoeffer's point is that if we do not listen to one another, soon we will no longer be listening to God either. He confidently claims this because Bonhoeffer was convinced that the primary way we encounter God is through our encounters with one another.[3]

---

2 Dietrich Bonhoeffer, *Life Together: The Classic Exploration of Christian Community* (New York: Harper & Row Publishers, 1954), 97.

3 Dietrich Bonhoeffer, "Sanctorum Communio," in *The Bonhoeffer Reader*, Clifford J. Green and Michael P. DeJonge, eds. (Minneapolis: Fortress Press, 2013), 27–28.

The way we encounter each other as we listen to others' stories as we tell our own is no ordinary encounter. Storytelling, which requires an audience who is actively listening, is a sacred act. It is a spiritual practice that is itself theological—even without some professional theologian chiming in.

Meaning Is Not Found, It Is Made

Throughout this project, I would often casually tell others that I was interested in how people find meaning and purpose in their working lives. Yet, embedded in the very words I used to describe what I was doing was a conceptual flaw. Everyday life does not contain hidden or lost meanings just waiting for us to stumble upon them. Rather, meaning must be created.

This shift from finding meaning to making meaning points to an important dynamic at play throughout my project and, I believe, for the future of theology. When I invited these ordinary workers to sit down with me for an interview, I was initiating an intervention. That is because everyday life itself is a daily grind and a struggle. It is a series of events and encounters that just never stop coming; it is one thing after another. And so we move through this daily grind in ways that are largely unreflective, guided by habits more than anything else. Hannah Arendt, whom I mentioned before, described this way of being as "the active life"—where our actions in a life often remain an enigma beyond our understanding. Often we do not know fully what we are doing.[4]

My questions, however, shifted participants into what Arendt called "the contemplative life," or in other words, a way of being that only in retrospect ascribes intention (or blame) and meaning, where previously there were only the raw materials of the active life. Of course, whether or not they agreed to sit down with me, they were already engaged in this contemplative way of being. We

---

4 Jackson, *The Politics of Storytelling*, 20–21.

cannot help but try to make sense of our everyday lives. And the most significant means we have for doing the work of meaning-making is telling stories.

As we tell stories about our lives, we become the authors of our own lives. But as so many of the stories we have heard make clear, we always do so within the limits of our abilities and the resources available to us. Our storytelling is a creative act, a means by which we make our lives intelligible to others, but it is also a coping mechanism—a strategy for surviving the daily grind of everyday life and taking back a measure of control when it feels as if life is happening *to* us rather than *because* of us.

Much more than an abstract set of beliefs or set of rules pre-scribing how to live one's life, Christianity is an entire repertoire of stories about God and God's people finding their way to one another. We are invited to discover that in our story repertoire too; that we are actually characters with significant subplots in a much bigger story about God's ongoing work in the world. And that story is yet unfinished, which I take to be very good news.

Unfortunately, you and I live in a time where the church is going through an interim time. "The old is not old enough to die, and the new is too young to be born," as the Irish poet John O'Donohue once described it.[5] Perhaps the new forms of church that are waiting to be born will be more like workshops or studios where we are invited to work on and work out our own stories. Perhaps there we will learn the repertoire of Christianity and learn how to improvise with it rather than merely rehearse the classics over and over again. Perhaps there we will find an ear that will listen, as Bonhoeffer said.

But until then, we may have to settle for something more ad hoc. We may have to create our own spaces for hearing and telling our stories at homes over dinners, in the break rooms at work,

---

5 John O'Donohue, "For Interim Time," in *To Bless the Space Between Us: A Book of Blessings* (New York: Doubleday, 2008), 119.

and in other cracks and crevices of daily life. We should do that. We should find ways to hear and tell more stories.

A Testimony

Within Christianity, *testimony* is a special genre of storytelling. It is a kind of first-person narrative that retells a story from everyday life in a way that reveals God at work. What follows is my own testimony of how listening to others' stories changed how I understand the meaning and purpose of my work as a theologian.

Part One: A Conversion

Before I set out on this project, one of my teachers and mentors—a sociologist by training—asked me point-blank how she could be sure I would handle the data I was collecting with integrity. Behind her question was a bit of history wherein theologians have not always followed the evidence wherever that evidence leads.

"Well, I want to be surprised," I blurted out loud. "If I am surprised by their stories. then I guess I can be sure, at some level, that I am not just paying attention to the stories I *want* to hear, but the ones that I *need* to hear."

She seemed satisfied with my answer, and just like that, I was off to a first round of interviews. Initially, I had thought I would do this project in New England, where I was living at the time, before my wife and I relocated to the Midwest. Before our big move, I sat down with a few people whose stories did not make it into these pages. One of those interviews surprised me in a way that caused me to rethink everything I thought I "knew" about vocation.

Late one morning in September, I took an Uber to an address where I expected to meet Roger. He had graciously agreed to participate in my project, but he said we would need to do the interview at his workplace over the lunch hour.

"Fine by me," I thought to myself.

My Uber pulled up to a nondescript office building with the street number prominently displayed on the reflective glass, which enveloped the entire structure. I walked in through the heavy metal and glass doors to find a few people dressed in business attire chatting with other colleagues in the lobby. I headed toward the large reception desk staffed with several security guards and gave them Roger's name. They made a call and then told me to take the elevator to the top floor. So I did.

As the door opened, Roger was waiting for me. He guided me through a maze of cubicles while explaining that his boss was not in today, so we could use her office for the interview. It would be quieter there, he said.

Roger's boss's office was a corner office with a stunning view. There was a desk in one corner, and in the opposite corner was a small table and two chairs flanked by bookcase on one side. The bookcase was basically a trophy case; it was filled with all kinds of plaques and awards. The one that stood out was a large medal with a dark blue ribbon pinned to a dark wooden plaque. On the plaque was a picture of a woman (Roger's boss) and President Barack Obama placing the medal around her neck. I gazed at it for a while before Roger told me that she had won the National Merit Award for Science as a part of her work mapping the human genome.

"Oh, that's casual," I thought to myself. As it turned out, Roger had managed his boss's laboratory for most of her career. When I asked him if he ever thought of this work as a calling, I felt silly even asking. Obviously he would. But to my surprise, he did not. "Oh no, I don't do the real science," he said.

For the next several weeks, I struggled with Roger's response to my question. He was clear that he did not think about his work as a vocation. He said that even though the wall behind him displayed all the evidence anyone would need to conclude that he was a part of developing new scientific breakthroughs that had all kinds of benefits for humankind. I thought it was obvious his work was a vocation; he absolutely did not.

Listening to Roger taught me that even if it was true that my training as a theologian helped me see and hear God at work, his own self-understanding is what mattered most. And this realization meant, at times, setting aside the urge to interject or reframe someone else's understanding of themselves and their work even if I had solid theological reasoning for doing so. Maybe it was not my job as a theologian to convince Roger to understand his work as a calling.

I have come to describe my interview with Roger as a conversion experience because it was the beginning of a shift from seeing the work of theology as a one-way street from tradition to everyday life to something more dynamic where theology may, at times, shape everyday life, or, more often, everyday life shapes theology. This, of course, was an important conversion for this project, but it has also changed the trajectory of all my theological work.

And it has changed how I see God at work through theology. I see God at work in the in-between, that is, in what occurs between the storyteller and the listener. God is certainly at work in the daily grind of our lives, although God's work there is often masked and challenging to see in the moment. But something special happens when we step back into "the contemplative life,"[6] as Arendt would call it, and revisit our own stories. This practice of retrospectively making meaning in our everyday lives is already theological. Psychoanalysts, spiritual directors, and good pastors have long known about the power of such storytelling, but we theologians have too often sheltered ourselves from it.

I, for one, am grateful for Roger and all the others who converted me to this alternative way of thinking about the purpose of theology.

---

6 Jackson, *The Politics of Storytelling*, 20.

Part Two: A Confession

If I am honest, I used to think that theology was special. Before I became a professional theologian, I had a somewhat romantic view of the work. I thought most of what I would do as a theologian was those things that I loved most about being a student of theology: writing, learning, teaching, and most of all, having meaningful conversations with interesting people about the things that matter most in our lives. I was not entirely wrong about the work. Those things *do* happen.

However, the work includes two other kinds of work that I did not have in mind when I set out to become a theologian. One, I did not anticipate the labyrinth of bureaucracy and minutiae that would take up more time than I imagined possible. Apparently, no job is without mind-numbing, nonsensical tasks that test the limits of human patience and fortitude. Two, I did not anticipate the self-work. Perhaps that part of this confession will come across as naïve or drenched with privilege. I accept that those impressions are likely accurate. Taken together, these are what make our work difficult and laborious.

Above I described how each of us learn to play by different "rules of the game" at work, home, church, and so on. That reality is what makes our working lives different from one another. Yet, it is worth pointing out that much of what our working lives have in common are these difficult matters: those things at work that we must simply endure and those things that invite us to work on ourselves. The workers who participated in this project taught me that this self-work is a significant part of the meaning of our work. It is a part of work that is difficult to avoid, and on this front, theologians are not special. We do not get a pass. We, too, must answer, somehow, the existential questions our work asks of us. Consider the following questions:

What can I do/contribute? This question is about the knowledge, gifts, and skills one brings to their work. During the year

I spent listening to these workers, I heard a lot of stories that explored this question. James (city planner) had been taking things apart and putting them back together his whole life. He knew he had the gifts to be an engineer, but he also needed the specialized knowledge and credentials his formal education provided. Mary tried to not be a hairdresser, but time and again she returned to it because it is what she knew. Laura (chiropractor) had to delay her dream of being a doctor but returned to this question after the sudden death of her husband.

These stories of struggling to answer this question—*what I contribute*—were a reminder that this project was the final crucible on my way to becoming a professional theologian. My own ability to answer this question would largely depend on whether I had anything meaningful to say about all these interviews. The irony of this was not lost on me. Still, in a strange way, I found it comforting to know this question was, for many, a lifelong pursuit.

Will anyone else value my work? It is one thing to have some marketable skills, but it is quite another to find others who will genuinely value your work. Sally (operations manager) is, perhaps, the best example of this. It's not that the church did not value her work, but her gifts and skills were simply *more valuable* elsewhere. And Ben (casket maker) reminded me that some people will readily accept a lower-paying job if it means working at a place that treats you well.

Just as this project began, I took my first position at a seminary. By then, I was hearing horror story after horror story from my peers who were looking for jobs. The hiring process in higher education is long, inefficient, and often highly political. But I had gotten this position because of a chance encounter, followed by a conversation in an airport on the way home from a conference. It was tempting to believe that I avoided the gauntlet because I was special. The stories I heard from Sally, Ben, and others reminded me that more likely, it was simply a matter of chance.

Who am I at work? This question is about the identities we take on in our work. For some, who we are at work is among the most important identities we have. David (farmer) is a good example of that. Remember his declaration: "I was born to farm." However, Caroline (teacher and real estate agent) was clear that even though she *liked* teaching, her most important work was being a mom—an identity at the very core of her being.

Nearly every interview I conducted included some kind of struggle with this question. I found that reassuring because I too struggled with the question and then felt guilty about it. Identity work is complex because it is not just a matter of who you want to be or claim to be. It is also a matter of how others see you. Workers such as David and Caroline helped me see that this is an important question to struggle with, but we are not *only* who we are at work.

How will I and my work change over time? This question is grounded in the reality that most of us will be working for most of our lives. Leslie (human resources executive) has spent her entire career with one company. Yet, that hardly means she has not struggled to change her circumstances within that career. In fact, it was this very reality that drove her to ask God what her purpose really was there. Finding her spiritual purpose re-ignited her passion. Valerie (teacher trainer) discovered that not all change at work is for the better; it can go downhill, and it can do so fast.

I spent years and years preparing to become a professional theologian and embarrassingly never once considered the trajectory of that career. I was so concerned with getting started that I really never thought much about where, exactly, I would be going. Stories like Leslie's and Valerie's were a wake-up call that taught me that this is a question that we confront whether we want to or not.

What makes it worth it? We live in a culture where success at work is often defined for us. Yet, this question is anything but settled. One of the best parts of this project was hearing some surprising answers to this question. I did not expect to hear answers like Karl's (farmer and bus-driver) story about finding joy in twenty-four years of driving kids to school on the bus. Or answers like John's (meat department supervisor) story about mentoring colleagues through difficult divorces.

It was difficult to learn from these stories that much of what makes work worth it are *not* the things these workers anticipated. Even if I had not thought much about the trajectory of my career, I assumed I would look for the answer to this question in the book deals, the speaking engagements, getting tenure, and all the other benchmarks that scholars like me are supposed to care most about. Often in these stories, it was not the professional accomplishments, the six-figure jobs, or the next raise that answered this question. More often these workers found answers to this question in the unforeseen twists and turns. I am more ready now for the unexpected because of their stories.

In all my listening, I was quite hesitant in the moment to interject my own views and judgements into their stories. My job was to listen first. But here at the end, I can testify that I saw God most clearly at work as these workers confronted these existential questions.

What can I do/contribute?
Will anyone else value my work?
Who am I at work?
How will I and my work change over time?
What makes it worth it?

Like the practice of storytelling, these questions are already theological. The answers my participants had to these questions often did not look like the vocational script, or any other carefully crafted doctrine. Instead, their answers looked like something more well-worn, something woven out of the fabric of their everyday lives. They looked more like *lived* vocations, like stories of faith at work. And when I say they were "at work," I do not just mean that they showed up at their workplaces. Rather, they were stories that in their very telling were *at work* doing the work of theology.

Being on the receiving end of all these stories certainly strengthened my faith and changed how I think about my vocation. And that is why we need to tell more stories.

Acknowledgments

Writing is hard work, and I doubt I could have written even a single page without the help of others. The book you are holding is loosely based on research I conducted as part of my doctoral program at Boston University. That research was supervised by Mary Elizabeth Moore and Nancy Tatom Ammerman—two extraordinary scholars who were as generous as they were demanding. I am grateful for their guidance throughout the years it took to complete this work.

This book would never have seen the light of day were it not for my editor at Fortress Press, Scott Tunseth. Since this project had its origins in my dissertation research, I assumed its audience would be other academics. Only at Scott's encouragement did I begin to imagine the book you are holding. Throughout the process Scott has been endlessly patient as I learned to write a genre I had never written before. As this project concluded, Laura Gifford and Ryan Hemmer played important roles getting things over the finish line and I am very grateful for their partnership as well.

I am also grateful for my first cohort of doctor of ministry students at The General Theological Seminary, who inspired this "book of everyday stories." Their enthusiasm for listening to the voices of ordinary Christians convinced me that pastoral leaders needed to hear these stories. To Alison, Clelia, Ian, Marion, Nancy, Todd, Paul—thank you for teaching me as much as I have taught you.

I wrote this book while serving on the faculty of Wesley Theological Seminary. A special thanks to Doug Powe, director of The Lewis Center for Church Leadership, who generously provided space for my own research and writing. I am also grateful to my faculty colleagues who encouraged me along the way.

Several others generously provided feedback on early drafts, including Josh Guyer, Jason Davis, Tim Bauerkemper, Char Rochuy Cox, and Carrie Greenquist-Petersen. Their feedback helped me understand how pastors and lay leaders might encounter these stories. Ulrike Guthrie provided much-needed developmental editing during the writing process. The pages that follow are much better, thanks to her.

Finally, I am thankful for the support of my family—especially my wife, Lindsey Queener, who never once complained about the long evenings and weekends I spent away working on this project. She also read the complete draft, offering helpful questions, insights, and encouragement along the way. I have dedicated the book to my mother and father because not all work is paid; my brothers and I are their labor of love, and I owe so much to them that words alone could never suffice. Thanks Mom and Dad, I love you very much.

Bibliography

Vocation

Anderson, Mary Elizabeth. "Gustaf Wingren (1910–2000)." *Lutheran Quarterly* 23, no. 2 (2009): 198–217.

———. *Gustaf Wingren and the Swedish Luther Renaissance.* American University Studies 243. New York: Peter Lang, 2006.

Buechner, Frederick. *Wishful Thinking: A Theological ABC.* New York: Harper & Row, 1973.

Hagen, Kenneth George. "A Critique of Wingren on Luther on Vocation." *Lutheran Quarterly* 16, no. 3 (2002): 249–73.

Hendrix, Scott H. "Luther on Marriage." *Lutheran Quarterly* 14, no. 3 (2000): 335–50.

Keefe-Perry, L. Callid. "Called into Crucible: Vocation and Moral Injury in U.S. Public School Teachers." *Religious Education* 113, no. 5 (2018): 489–500.

Kolden, Marc. "Work and Meaning: Some Theological Reflections." *Interpretation* 48, no. 3 (1994): 262.

Nahnfeldt, Cecilia. "Vocation and Encounter: A Scandinavian Theological Reflection on Everyday Life as Christians." *Dialog* 57, no. 2 (2018): 91–98.

Pennington, M. Basil. *Called, New Thinking on Christian Vocation.* New York: Seabury Press, 1983.

Persaud, Winston D. "Luther on Vocation, by Gustaf Wingren: A Twenty-First-Century Theological-Literary Reading." *Dialog* 57, no. 2 (2018): 84–90.

Schuurman, Douglas James. *Vocation: Discerning Our Callings in Life*. Grand Rapids, MI: W.B. Eerdmans Publishing, 2004.

Snyder, Timothy. "Towards a New Agenda for Vocation." *Dialog* 60, no. 1 (2021): 72–78.

Stevens, R. Paul. *The Other Six Days: Vocation, Work, and Ministry in Biblical Perspective*. Grand Rapids, MI/Vancouver: W.B. Eerdmans Publishing/Regent College Pub, 1999.

Strohl, Jane E. "Marriage as Discipleship: Luther's Praise of Married Life." *Dialog* 47, no. 2 (2008): 136–42.

Tranvik, Mark D. *Martin Luther and the Called Life*. Minneapolis: Fortress Press, 2016.

Veith, Gene Edward. *God at Work: Your Christian Vocation in All of Life*. Wheaton, IL: Crossway Books, 2002.

Wingren, Gustaf. *Luther on Vocation*. Eugene, OR: Wipf & Stock Publishers, 2004.

Lutheran Theology

Bayer, Oswald. *Martin Luther's Theology: A Contemporary Interpretation*. Grand Rapids, MI: W. B. Eerdmans Publishing, 2008.

———. "Nature and Institution: Luther's Doctrine of the Three Orders." *Lutheran Quarterly* 12, no. 2 (1998): 125–59.

Bielfeldt, Dennis. "Luther on Language." *Lutheran Quarterly* 16, no. 2 (2002): 195–220.

Forde, Gerhard O. *On Being a Theologian of the Cross: Reflections on Luther's Heidelberg Disputation, 1518*. Grand Rapids, MI: W. B. Eerdmans Publishing, 1997.

Kolb, Robert, and Timothy J. Wengert, eds. *The Book of Concord: The Confessions of the Evangelical Lutheran Church*. Translated by Charles Arand, Eric Gritsch, Robert Kolb, William Russell, James Schaaf, Jane Strohl, and Timothy J. Wengert. Minneapolis: Fortress Press, 2000.

Lazareth, William H. *Luther on the Christian Home: An Application of the Social Ethics of the Reformation*. Philadelphia: Muhlenberg Press, 1960.

Lindbeck, George A. *The Nature of Doctrine: Religion and Theology in a Postliberal Age*. Philadelphia: Westminster Press, 1984.

Luther, Martin. *Career of the Reformer I*. Edited by Harold John Grimm. American Edition, vol. 31. Luther's Works. Philadelphia: Muhlenberg Press, 1957.

———. *Career of the Reformer III*. Edited by Philip S. Watson. American Edition, vol. 33. Luther's Works. Philadelphia: Fortress Press, 1972.

———. *Commentaries on 1 Corinthians 7, 1 Corinthians 15, Lectures on 1 Timothy*. Edited by Hilton C. Oswald. American Edition, vol. 28. Luther's Works. Saint Louis: Concordia Publishing House, 1973.

———. *Lectures on Galatians, 1535: Chapters 1–4*. Edited by Jaroslav Pelikan and Walter A. Hansen. American Edition, vol. 26. Luther's Works. Saint Louis: Concordia Publishing House, 1963.

———. *Lectures on Romans: Glosses and Scholia*. Edited by Hilton C. Oswald. American Edition, vol. 25. Luther's Works. Saint Louis: Concordia Publishing House, 1972.

———. *Letters II*. Edited by Gottfried Krodel. American Edition, vol. 49. Luther's Works. Saint Louis: Concordia Publishing House, 1972.

———. *The Christian in Society I*. Edited by James Atkinson. American Edition, vol. 44. Luther's Works. Saint Louis: Concordia Publishing House, 1966.

———. *The Christian in Society III*. Edited by Robert C. Schultz. American Edition, vol. 46. Luther's Works. Saint Louis: Concordia Publishing House, 1967.

———. *Word and Sacrament I.* Edited by E. Theodore Bachmann. American Edition, vol. 35. Luther's Works. Saint
Louis, Mo.: Concordia Publishing House, 1960.

Streufert, Mary J., ed. *Transformative Lutheran Theologies: Femi-
nist, Womanist, and Mujerista Perspectives.* Minneapolis:
Fortress Press, 2010.

Wengert, Timothy J., ed. *Harvesting Martin Luther's Reflections
on Theology, Ethics, and the Church.* Grand Rapids, MI:
W. B. Eerdmans Publishing, 2004.

———, ed. *The Pastoral Luther: Essays on Martin Luther's Practical Theology.* Lutheran Quarterly Books. Grand Rapids,
MI: W. B. Eerdmans Publishing, 2009.

Theologies of Work

Arnal, Oscar L. *Priests in Working-Class Blue: The History of the
Worker-Priests (1943–1954).* New York: Paulist Press,
1986.

Banks, Robert. *Faith Goes to Work: Reflections from the Marketplace.* Eugene, OR: Wipf & Stock Publishers, 2000.

Bell, George K. A. *The Stockholm Conference, 1925: The
Official Report of the Universal Christian Confer-
ence on Life and Work Held in Stockholm, 19–30
August, 1925.* New York: Oxford University Press/H.
Milford, 1926.

Catholic Church, and John Paul II. *Laborem Exercens: On
Human Work.* Washington, DC: Office for Publishing
and Promotion Services, United States Catholic Conference, 1981.

Chenu, Marie-Dominique. *The Theology of Work: An Exploration.* Translated by Lilian Soiron. Chicago: Henry Regnery, 1966.

Cosden, Darrell. *A Theology of Work: Work and the New Creation.*
Eugene, OR: Wipf & Stock, 2006.

Diefer, Gregor. *The Church and Industrial Society: A Survey of the Worker-Priest Movement and Its Implications for the Christian Mission.* Translated by Isabel and Florence McHugh. London: Darton, Longman and Todd, 1964.

Ellul, Jacques. "Work and Calling." *Katallagete* 4, no. 10 (Fall 1972): 8–16.

Fox, Matthew. *The Reinvention of Work: A New Vision of Livelihood for Our Time.* San Francisco: Harper San Francisco, 1994.

Hardy, Lee. *The Fabric of This World: Inquiries into Calling, Career Choice, and the Design of Human Work.* Grand Rapids, MI: W. B. Eerdmans Publishing, 1990.

Knapp, John C. *How the Church Fails Businesspeople: And What Can Be Done about It.* Grand Rapids, MI: W. B. Eerdmans Publishing, 2012.

Larive, Armand. *After Sunday: A Theology of Work.* New York: Continuum, 2004.

Martin, Joan M. *More than Chains and Toil: A Christian Work Ethic of Enslaved Women.* Louisville, KY: Westminster John Knox Press, 2000.

Miller-McLemore, Bonnie J. *Also a Mother: Work and Family as Theological Dilemma.* Nashville: Abingdon Press, 1994.

Palmer, Parker J. *The Active Life: A Spirituality of Work, Creativity, and Caring.* San Francisco: Harper & Row, 1990.

Sweeden, Joshua R., and Michael Cartwright. *The Church and Work: The Ecclesiological Grounding of Good Work.* Eugene, OR: Pickwick Publications, 2014.

Volf, Miroslav. *Work in the Spirit: Toward a Theology of Work.* Eugene, OR: Wipf & Stock Publishers, 2001.

Witherington, Ben. *Work: A Kingdom Perspective on Labor.* Grand Rapids, MI: W. B. Eerdmans Publishing, 2011.

Everyday Religion and Lived Theology

Ammerman, Nancy Tatom, ed. *Everyday Religion: Observing Modern Religious Lives*. New York: Oxford University Press, 2007.

————. *Sacred Stories, Spiritual Tribes: Finding Religion in Everyday Life*. New York: Oxford University Press, 2014.

Astley, Jeff. *Ordinary Theology: Looking, Listening, and Learning in Theology*. Explorations in Practical, Pastoral, and Empirical Theology. Burlington, VT: Ashgate, 2002.

Astley, Jeff, and Leslie J. Francis, eds. *Exploring Ordinary Theology: Everyday Christian Believing and the Church*. Explorations in Practical, Pastoral and Empirical Theology. Burlington, VT: Ashgate, 2013.

Diehl, William E. *Christianity and Real Life*. Philadelphia: Fortress Press, 1976.

————. *Monday Connection: On Being an Authentic Christian in a Weekday World*. Eugene, OR: Wipf & Stock Publishers, 2012.

Marsh, Charles, ed. *Lived Theology: New Perspectives on Method, Style, and Pedagogy*. New York: Oxford University Press, 2017.

McGuire, Meredith B. *Lived Religion: Faith and Practice in Everyday Life*. New York: Oxford University Press, 2008.

Storytelling

Gottschall, Jonathan. *The Storytelling Animal: How Stories Make Us Human*. Boston: Mariner Books, 2012.

Jackson, Michael. *The Politics of Storytelling: Variations on a Theme by Hannah Arendt*. 2nd ed. Critical Anthropology, vol. 3. Copenhagen: Museum Musculanum Press/ University of Copenhagen, 2013.

McAdams, Dan P. *The Stories We Live by: Personal Myths and the Making of the Self*. New York: Guilford Press, 1997.

McClendon, James William. *Biography as Theology: How Life Stories Can Remake Today's Theology*. Eugene, OR: Wipf & Stock Publishers, 2002.

Additional Reading

Graeber, David. *Bullshit Jobs: A Theory*. New York: Simon & Schuster, 2018.

Isay, Dave. *Callings: The Purpose and Passion of Work*. New York: Penguin Books, 2017.

Lucassen, Jan. *The Story of Work: A New History of Humankind*. New Haven: Yale University Press, 2021.

Miller, David W. *God at Work: The History and Promise of the Faith at Work Movement*. New York: Oxford University Press, 2007.

Press, Eyal. *Dirty Work: Essential Jobs and the Hidden Toll of Inequality in America*. New York: Parrar, Straus and Giroux, 2021.

Terkel, Studs. *Hard Times: An Oral History of the Great Depression*. New York: New Press, 2000.

———. *Working: People Talk About What They Do All Day and How They Feel About What They Do*. New York: New Press, 2004.

Weber, Max. *The Protestant Ethic and the Spirit of Capitalism with Other Writings on the Rise of the West*. Translated by Stephen Kalberg. 4th ed. New York: Oxford University Press, 2002.